UNLOCKI... THE SECRETS OF WEB 3.0 WEALTH

YOUR GUIDE TO DECENTRALIZED FINANCE In...

2028

Master Defi: Insider strategies, step-by-step guidance, and tools to grow your wealth in the Web3 era

Web 3.0 Full Stack Developer & DeFi Expert

BIT MAIN STREET MARKET

Table of Contents

The Author

Dedication

Why I Wrote This Book

New Opening Option: The Awakening

Chapter 1: Introduction to Web 3.0 - The Foundation of Digital Revolution

Chapter 2: Technological Foundations of Web 3.0 - The Infrastructure of Freedom

Chapter 3: Unlocking the Secrets - The Great Deception Unveiled

Chapter 4: The Hidden Architecture - DeFi Fundamentals Revealed

Chapter 5: The Underground Economy - Current DeFi Ecosystem Exposed

Chapter 6: The Security Codes - Protection Secrets They Don't Want You to Know

Chapter 7: The Legal Labyrinth - Regulatory Secrets and Compliance Codes

Chapter 8: The Master's Playbook - Advanced DeFi Strategies Unveiled

Chapter 9: The Sovereign Network - Building Your Web 3.0 Empire

Chapter 10: Step-by-Step DeFi Setup Guide - Your Complete 2028 Implementation Roadmap

BONUS SECTION: Special Edition Reference Materials

Complete DeFi Glossary: Your A-Z Guide to Decentralized Finance

References and Resources

Conclusion

About the Author

UNLOCKING THE SECRETS OF WEB 3.0 WEALTH

David James Green

Published by BIT MAIN STREET MEDIA, 2025.

UNLOCKING THE SECRETS OF WEB 3.0 WEALTH

First edition. August 17, 2025.

ISBN: 979-8218747541

Publisher: Bit Main Street Media
Written by David James Green.

"*While they work on building followers, we build communities. While they create content, we create the protocols. While they place trust in others' platforms, we become the platform. While they compete for attention, we architect abundance.*"

- The Sovereign Network Manifesto

UNLOCKING THE SECRETS OF WEB 3.0 WEALTH

Your Guide to Decentralized Finance for 2025 Through 2028

Master DeFi: Insider strategies, step-by-step guidance, and tools to grow your wealth in the Web3 era.

DAVID JAMES GREEN

BITMAINSTREET.COM

The Author

HELLO, MY NAME IS DAVID,

founder of Bit Main Street, creator of Satoshi For Storage, and a man on a mission to help everyday people become extraordinary through the power of decentralized technology.

With over 25 years of experience as a full-stack .NET developer, I've spent my life building digital systems that break boundaries not reinforce them. My journey began in the Bay Area, where I sharpened my technical craft in Silicon Valley during the early web revolution. That journey took me across the world, where I worked with global financial institutions like Saxo Bank and Citigroup in Copenhagen, Denmark, helping to develop high-performance digital platforms that powered international banking operations.

But my roots run deeper than code.

I'm also a certified martial artist trained in Peace Power Qigong under Master Fan Xiulan, a practice rooted in discipline, energy, and focus. The same principles that guide my physical training fuel my approach to technology: precision, balance, and respect for the unseen forces at play. Whether in the dojo or the digital world, my aim has always been the same: liberation through mastery.

Over the years, I've grown from software engineer to crypto educator, entrepreneur, and community builder. I founded the Crypto Academy and launched the Bit Main Street Network to empower entrepreneurs with tools, training, and decentralized solutions that actually work. My clients aren't just learning; they're transforming their businesses into sovereign ecosystems.

One of my proudest innovations is Satoshi For Storage, a privacy-first, Bitcoin-powered file hosting system that combines IPFS security with Lightning payments. No surveillance. No middlemen. Just speed, freedom, and control: the way the internet was always meant to be.

If you're ready to be transformed, then your teacher has arrived, and I've never backed down from the truth.

Dedication

First and foremost, I give thanks to **AHYAH** for the spiritual guidance and divine inspiration that led me to write this book. My foundation in faith keeps me grounded, lights my path, and reveals insight into what's coming in our near future.

This book is dedicated to my dear friend and the mother of my two beautiful boys, Jessica, and to my sons Elias and Benjamin Green, you are my legacy and my reason.

To the most powerful individual I've ever met, a true angel on Earth, my sister, Tina M. Johnson, your strength and spirit are unmatched.

To my childhood friend and brother from another mother, Rafael Diaz, thank you for the countless hours of uplifting conversation that kept me focused and inspired.

To my brother Stephen Petties, my sister Princess Petties, and your beautiful family, your love and unity are a blessing.

And to my mother, Mozel, for always offering words of encouragement and unwavering support you planted this seed in me.

This book is dedicated to you. With love, honor, and purpose.

Why I Wrote This Book

I wrote this book because I saw too many people getting left behind in a digital economy that was supposed to set us free. I watched misinformation flood on the internet, scammers hijack the conversation, and good people miss out on generational opportunities.

These days, the question keeps coming up: "Why did you build it?" or "What problem are you trying to solve?" The answer is simple the problem is poverty, and the growing wealth gap that continues to divide our communities.

But I believe we can solve this problem. Not by waiting on permission... but by building together. One mind, one move, one lesson at a time. As the old saying goes: **each one, teach one**.

And with this book, I will teach you not just how to navigate Web 3.0, but how to thrive in it. Web 3.0 isn't just the future it's the now for those bold enough to tap into it. My mission is simple: to break down the complexity, expose the real truth behind decentralized tech, and equip you with the tools to become more than just a participant to become a creator of wealth in this new digital era.

This isn't just another crypto how-to. It's a blueprint for freedom. Let's break the chains and unlock the wealth that's been waiting for us. **Let's get to work.**

Table of Contents

The Author

Dedication

Why I Wrote This Book

New Opening Option: The Awakening

Chapter 1: Introduction to Web 3.0 - The Foundation of Digital Revolution

Chapter 2: Technological Foundations of Web 3.0 - The Infrastructure of Freedom

Chapter 3: Unlocking the Secrets - The Great Deception Unveiled

Chapter 4: The Hidden Architecture - DeFi Fundamentals Revealed

Chapter 5: The Underground Economy - Current DeFi Ecosystem Exposed

Chapter 6: The Security Codes - Protection Secrets They Don't Want You to Know

Chapter 7: The Legal Labyrinth - Regulatory Secrets and Compliance Codes

Chapter 8: The Master's Playbook - Advanced DeFi Strategies Unveiled

Chapter 9: The Sovereign Network - Building Your Web 3.0 Empire

Chapter 10: Step-by-Step DeFi Setup Guide - Your Complete 2028 Implementation Roadmap

BONUS SECTION: Special Edition Reference Materials

Complete DeFi Glossary: Your A-Z Guide to Decentralized Finance

References and Resources

Conclusion

About the Author

New Opening Option: The Awakening

THE LAST TIME THIS HAPPENED

In 1849, the California Gold Rush created exactly 3,000 documented gold millionaires.

It created over 15,000 millionaires selling picks, shovels, and jeans.

In 1999, the Internet boom saw 10,000 websites launch daily.

But 90% of the wealth went to those who built the infrastructure—the servers, the payment rails, the protocols.

Today, in 2025, millions chase tokens and NFT moonshots.

The real wealth is being built one layer deeper in the protocols that power it all.

History doesn't repeat. But it rhymes.

And you're holding the pickaxe.

IN THE NUMBERS

THE CREATOR ECONOMY TRUTH:

- 68% of part-time creators earn under $1,000 per YEAR
- 46% of FULL-TIME creators earn under poverty wages
- Platform take rate: 15-45% of everything you make
- Creator burnout: 78% quit within 24 months
- Average time to first dollar: 6-12 months
- Creators who become millionaires: 0.03%

THE PROTOCOL ECONOMY REALITY:

- Entry-level protocol developers: $100,000+ base salary
- Smart contract engineers: $250,000-$500,000 total comp
- Protocol revenue share: 100% (minus only network fees)
- Passive income potential: Protocols earn while you sleep

- Time to first revenue: Often immediate upon deployment
- Builders creating lasting wealth: 73%

One model turns you into a digital hamster on a wheel.

The other turns you into a digital landlord collecting rent.

Choose wisely.

Chapter 1

Introduction to Web 3.0 - The Foundation of Digital Revolution

"Web 3.0 will be decentralized, trustless, and permissionless. It will empower users to control their own data and participate in a truly global digital economy."

- Vitalik Buterin, Co-founder of Ethereum

The most exciting time of my life had to be between 2016 and October 2017, the moment ETH hit $300. I had never experienced the feeling of having no more financial worries. The new kid on the block was biting at Bitcoin's heels, the fork wars were raging, and the wild west of crypto was in full swing. This was the ICO era, when people became millionaires literally overnight. It felt like watching history happen in real time and being part of the script.

Nearly a decade later, millions of tokens, blockchains, and protocols flooded the market, but only a few have stood the test of time. Ethereum is still at the top of the list alongside Bitcoin, and what makes this technology so appealing is how it captures value at the protocol level. Think about it: the TCP/IP protocols form the transportation layer of the internet. The value of the internet protocol suite came alive in the application layer the layer that built Google, Facebook, Apple, Amazon, and the other so-called "FANG" giants. Ethereum works the same way, except instead of moving data, it moves value. But before I get too far ahead of myself, let's rewind and see how we got here.

The internet has come a long way since its inception, evolving through distinct phases that have reshaped how we live, work, and interact. It all began with Web 1.0, a static and information-centric era where users were mere consumers of content. This was the age of simple websites, email communication, and early search engines a digital library where you could read but not write. Then came Web 2.0, a revolutionary shift that turned the internet into a dynamic, user-driven ecosystem. Social media platforms, blogs, and wikis flourished, empowering users to create, share, and interact like never before.

With the rapid growth of the internet, we are on the cusp of another transformative phase: Web 3.0. This next generation of the internet promises to redefine how we interact online, emphasizing decentralization, user control, and privacy. Unlike previous versions, Web 3.0 aims to dismantle the centralized power structures that dominate today's internet, giving control back to the people through technologies like blockchain, cryptocurrencies, and decentralized applications (dApps).

Imagine a digital world where you truly own your data, where every transaction is transparent and secure, and where financial security and cyber-crimes are no longer looming threats. It will be a safe, self-directed digital world one where you set your own standards, define your own terms, and operate without hidden gatekeepers.

Web 3.0 isn't just the next version of the internet; it's a philosophical shift from merely connecting people to empowering them.

But to understand why Web 3.0 matters and why the struggle for digital freedom is so important we need to pull back the curtain on how we got here.

The first Secret we will unveil is The Hidden History of Internet Control. Most people know of the internet, but few know its true origin story. The public narrative skips over the fact that the internet was born inside the walls of DARPA the U.S. Defense Advanced Research Projects Agency. Long before social networks, streaming video, or search engines, this network was designed not for mass consumption, but for military communication, surveillance, and control.

In the dark corners of declassified history, we find that Web 1.0's first breath wasn't about connecting the world, it was about securing command.

Evolution of the Web: How Did It Start?

SECRET #1: The Hidden History of Internet Control

Web 1.0: The Foundation

And yet, while the military held the blueprint, the public only met the internet through its first major evolution: Web 1.0. Official history credits Tim Berners-Lee, a British computer scientist, with creating the World Wide Web in 1989. Building on the hypertext concepts introduced in 1963 by Ted Nelson, Berners-Lee not only programmed the first browser, but also developed the Hypertext Markup Language (HTML) and the Hypertext Transfer Protocol (HTTP). These tools told browsers how to display content and how web servers should deliver files laying the groundwork for everything that came after.

Berners-Lee even imagined a "Semantic Web" a system where data could link and interact across pages intelligently, but hardware limitations of the time kept this vision from becoming reality. Still, that early dream of interconnected, intelligent data would later become a cornerstone of Web 3.0.

The public's first real taste of the internet came in 1993 with the release of Mosaic, the first widely popular browser. It was quickly followed by Netscape Navigator, Microsoft Internet

Explorer, and later Apple Safari. Search engines like Yahoo! Search, Lycos, and AltaVista made the web navigable, though by 2004, Google had crushed most competitors and claimed the search crown. The "information superhighway" had officially opened but few realized that the toll booths were still manned by the same old gatekeepers.

SECRET #2: The Centralization Trap of Web 2.0

How Big Tech Captured the Internet

By the early 2000s, the web was no longer just a static library. The rise of blogging platforms, forums, and wikis gave people the power to share knowledge and connect across borders. This was the dawn of Web 2.0, the interactive, social internet. It promised a more democratic web where users weren't just consumers but creators, where anyone could publish their voice to the world.

But here's the catch: while people were busy uploading photos, posting blogs, and connecting with friends, a new kind of empire was being built in the background. Meta,

Twitter, Google, and Amazon didn't just offer services they became the gatekeepers of the digital age. They owned the servers, controlled the algorithms, and decided what content thrived and what disappeared. Web 2.0 brought people together, but it also concentrated unimaginable power in the hands of a few corporations.

This was the golden age of "free" free email, free search, free social media but the price was hidden in plain sight. If you weren't paying for the product, you were the product. Every post, like, and search became data to be mined, sold, and weaponized for profit.

This is the centralization trap: the illusion of freedom while operating inside walled gardens you don't control. And it's exactly the trap that Web 3.0 is designed to break.

SECRET #3: The 2028 Web 3.0 Wealth Explosion

Why Now Is the Perfect Time to Position Yourself

If Web 1.0 was the blueprint and Web 2.0 was the takeover, Web 3.0 is the jailbreak. This third generation of the World Wide Web is all about taking back the keys, putting you in control of your data, your identity, and your wealth. Instead of logging into someone else's platform and handing over your life story, Web 3.0 lets you operate on your own terms, with your assets, your data, and your rules protected by blockchain technology.

The term "Web3" was coined in 2014 by Gavin Wood, co-founder of Ethereum and founder of Polkadot. Gavin saw what many didn't that centralized platforms were quietly becoming digital landlords. His vision for Web3 was a decentralized online ecosystem where no one entity could pull the plug on your life's work or lock you out of your own digital property. In Web 3.0, your wallet is your passport, your signature is your key, and your transactions are transparent, secure, and verifiable by anyone.

And here's why this matters now: the 2028 Bitcoin halving will collide with the global shift toward decentralized finance, setting the stage for one of the biggest wealth transfers in history. The infrastructure is maturing, the tools are becoming user-friendly, and the demand for alternatives to centralized systems is hitting critical mass.

The next five years aren't just about adopting new technology they're about positioning yourself to own a piece of the future's foundation. Miss this wave, and you might be watching from the shore as others sail into a new digital gold rush.

The Technical Foundation of Web 3.0

Web 3.0 isn't just a concept it's built on specific technologies:

Blockchain is the native state layer that solves Web 2.0's biggest flaw: the stateless nature of HTTP.

DeFi (Decentralized Finance) the beating heart of Web 3.0's economy, enabling transactions without banks or gatekeepers.

Crypto Wallets your access point to the decentralized web, holding everything from currency to NFTs.

NFTs unique digital assets tied directly to your wallet, representing anything from art to identity documents.

Decentralized Storage & Protocols IPFS for file storage, Whisper for secure messaging, Polkadot for blockchain interoperability, The Graph for indexing blockchain data, and Filecoin for storage marketplaces.

Each of these isn't just "tech" they're weapons in the fight for digital sovereignty.

The Metaverse Connection

The metaverse is the immersive frontier, a virtual space where AR, VR, and MR create 3D worlds you can walk through. Built right, it's an extension of Web 3.0's decentralized promise. Built wrong, it's another walled garden.

Web 3.0 technologies can ensure metaverses are interoperable, censorship-resistant, and owned by the communities that build them. Without that, the metaverse will be the same old trap in a shinier box.

Web 2.0 vs. Web 3.0: The Battle for Control

Web 2.0 Centralized, controlled, ad-driven, data-mining empires.

Web 3.0 Decentralized, user-owned, blockchain-secured economies.

The difference isn't just technical, it's philosophical. Web 2.0 connects people under corporate rules. Web 3.0 connects people under their own rules.

Where It's All Going

Web 3.0 will be everywhere embedded in IoT devices, smart cities, vehicles and wearables. It's not tied to a desktop or even a phone. It's omnipresent. And beyond it? Web 4.0 AI-driven, hyper-personalized, fully immersive is already on the horizon.

You're not just reading about the future. You're standing at the door. And the next chapters will hand you the keys.

The Market Opportunity Is Staggering:

The global Web 3.0 market experienced rapid growth, with a valuation of USD 1.76 billion in 2023. However, this market is projected to expand significantly, rising from USD 2.55 billion in 2024 to an impressive USD 49.88 billion by 2032. This remarkable growth reflects a compound annual growth rate (CAGR) of 45.0% during the forecast period.

This surge in market size underscores the transformative potential of Web 3.0 technologies and their increasing adoption across various industries. By 2028, when the Bitcoin halving occurs and institutional adoption peaks, we're looking at the perfect storm for Web 3.0 wealth creation.

Web 3.0: The Decentralized Revolution

Blockchain technology offers a solution to one of the major challenges of Web 2.0: the stateless nature of the HTTP protocol. In Web3, blockchain serves as a native state layer, allowing it to store and transfer users' states (such as browsing history, favorites, and online purchases) independently of tech companies. This means that users can maintain control over their data without relying on centralized entities.

Imagine planning a vacation on a tight budget. Right now, you'd likely spend countless hours scouring the internet for the best deals on flights, accommodation, and car rentals. It's a tedious process, bouncing between different websites, comparing prices, and trying to find the perfect combination that fits your budget.

But with Web 3.0, things are about to get a whole lot easier. Picture this: intelligent search engines or bots, that can do all the hard work for you. Instead of manually sifting through endless options, these smart tools will analyze your preferences and profile and then sift through a vast array of data to generate tailored recommendations just for you.

The DeFi Connection: Your Gateway to Web 3.0 Wealth

Decentralized finance (DeFi) is a cornerstone of Web 3.0, offering a suite of technologies that enable cryptocurrencies and blockchain to function in digital environments. With DeFi, users can conduct financial operations like sending, receiving, and exchanging money without the need for traditional banks or government oversight. This decentralization effectively shifts power away from Big Tech companies and financial institutions.

Think of blockchain as a natural extension of the internet protocol, enabling users to preserve their history and current state without the need for storing local cookies or relying on centralized servers. When a user connects to the internet from a new device, the system automatically transfers their state, ensuring a seamless and decentralized user experience across different devices and platforms.

Web 3.0 and the Metaverse: The Complete Digital Transformation

Web 3.0 and the metaverse are two distinct but often interrelated concepts, both envisioning a future of digital experiences that are decentralized and immersive. The metaverse represents a new paradigm for using the internet, transforming the traditional 2D web into an immersive three-dimensional virtual space. Instead of interacting through desktops and mobile screens, users can enter this virtual reality using VR glasses.

Web 3.0 shares similarities and differences with the metaverse in terms of function, operation, and applications. The metaverse can be built on Web 3.0's decentralized internet. While multiple metaverses can be created by different organizations, Web 3.0 can facilitate interoperability between them.

The Path to 2028: Why This Matters for Your Wealth

As we approach 2028 and the next Bitcoin halving, understanding Web 3.0 becomes crucial for wealth creation. The experience of Web 3.0 will be available everywhere, anytime. Gone are the days when the internet was confined to your desktop computer (Web 1.0) or even just your smartphone (Web 2.0). Web 3.0 will transcend these limitations, offering an omnipresent digital landscape.

With the proliferation of connected devices through the Internet of Things (IoT), Web 3.0 could rightfully be called the "web of everything and everywhere." Virtually everything around, you will be seamlessly integrated into the online world. From your household appliances to your car, from wearable devices to smart city infrastructure, the web will pervade every aspect of our lives.

This all-encompassing connectivity will not only redefine how we interact with technology but also revolutionize our relationship with the world around us. As Web 3.0 unfolds, it promises to empower individuals and communities by fostering a truly interconnected and immersive digital experience that transcends physical boundaries.

The future of Web 3.0 offers an intriguing glimpse into a new era of the internet, where advanced technologies seamlessly integrate to create a more intelligent and interconnected digital ecosystem. Understanding these foundations now positions you perfectly for the unprecedented wealth opportunities coming in 2028.

The clock is ticking. The foundation is being laid. And in the next chapter, we'll pull back the curtain on **the exact technological building blocks that make Web 3.0 possible** — and how you can start using them before the rest of the world catches on.

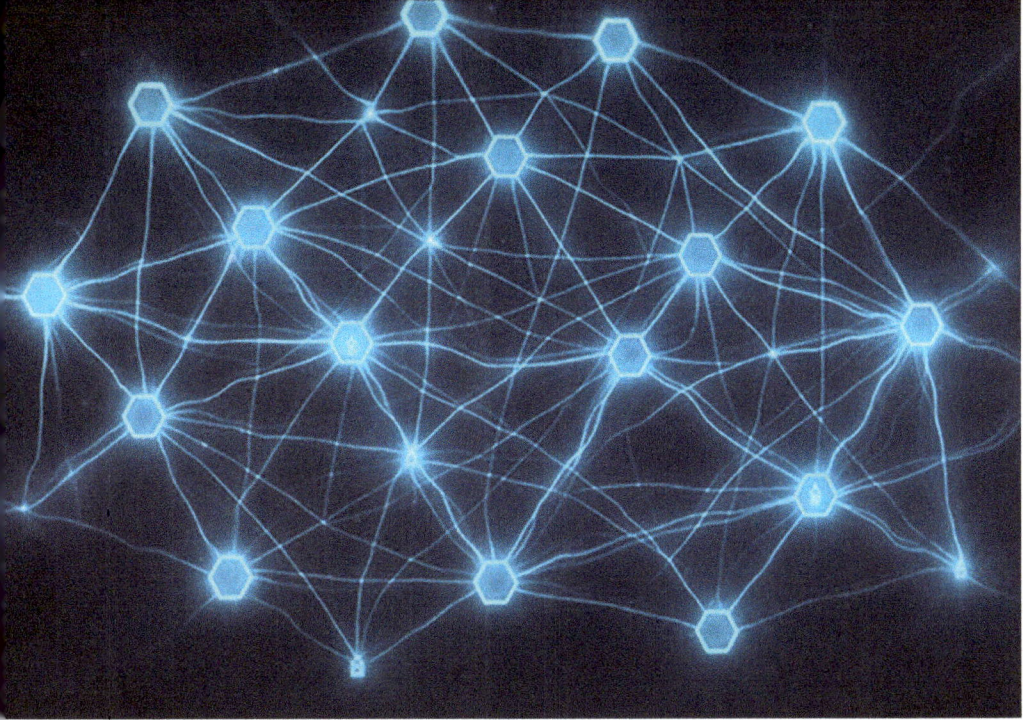

Chapter 2

Technological Foundations of Web 3.0 - The Infrastructure of Freedom

"The infrastructure we build today determines the freedom we'll have tomorrow."

Ever wondered about the technological foundations behind Web 3.0? It's like the engine powering the next level of our online experience. It will give us an internet where you, not some faceless corporation, call the shots on your own data, identity, and future.

That's the dream we're chasing. And like any revolution, it starts by understanding the tools. These are the blueprints and battle plans drawn up by the brightest minds and boldest innovators in blockchain, decentralization, AI, and next-gen networking.

For those who grasp these technologies first, the reward isn't just knowledge it's positioning. In a market racing toward a multi-trillion-dollar future, knowing how the infrastructure works gives you the power to build on it, profit from it, and protect your stake in it.

SECRET #4: The DeFi Foundation That Never Breaks

Web 3.0 Technologies: The Unbreakable Infrastructure

Web 3, or Decentralized Finance, represents one of the prominent sectors in the evolving landscape of Web 3.0 technologies. It seeks to transform the financial industry by eliminating the necessity of centralized authorities such as banks and payment processors, shifting towards a peer-to-peer financial system anchored on blockchain technology.

Proponents of DeFi envision a future where fees are reduced, transaction speeds are accelerated, and capital allocation becomes more efficient. Transparency is a key feature, as all transaction data, including loan amounts and collateral, is openly available on publicly accessible blockchains. Crucially, DeFi promises enhanced accessibility, enabling anyone with an internet connection to participate without cumbersome paperwork or reliance on third-party verifications.

Advocates argue that DeFi protocols like Uniswap (UNI), Aave (AAVE), and Chainlink (LINK) can replicate many of the services provided by traditional financial intermediaries, including banking services, lending and borrowing, asset trading, and insurance. This is why they survived when centralized exchanges like FTX collapsed, as we'll explore in the next chapters.

SECRET #5: The Semantic Web's Hidden Intelligence

How Machines Will Think Like Humans by 2028

If DeFi is the unbreakable financial foundation of Web 3.0, the **Semantic Web** is its brain — the hidden intelligence layer that will make the decentralized internet think like a human.

Often seen as a precursor to Web 3.0, the Semantic Web was designed to solve one of the internet's biggest problems: information overload without true understanding. It's not just about *finding* data — it's about linking, structuring, and contextualizing it so machines can interpret meaning, not just keywords.

At its core is the **Resource Description Framework (RDF), a neutral** data model that describes relationships between subjects (like a webpage) and objects (like the resources it links to). RDF doesn't care what syntax is used; it focuses on mapping connections, the way a detective draws lines between clues on a wall.

Building on that is the **Web Ontology Language (OWL),** a set of tools for defining ontologies — structured vocabularies that tell machines how concepts relate to each other. Think of it as teaching AI not just words, but how those words fit into the bigger picture. Out of this work, **Knowledge Graphs (KGs)** emerge vast, interconnected webs of entities and attributes, creating the blueprint for machine reasoning.

And here's a real-world, right-now example of how fast this is accelerating: **ChatGPT-5** has just been released. It's not just a conversational chatbot — it's a real-time reasoning engine that can parse, connect, and contextualize massive amounts of information across domains. GPT-5's leap forward from its predecessors shows us exactly where we're headed: AI systems that don't just answer questions, but *understand* context, integrate live data, and act as intelligent agents in complex ecosystems.

By 2028, these same principles will be hardwired into the Semantic Web powering AI-driven DeFi protocols that can scan global economic trends, social sentiment, and blockchain transactions in real time. They'll deploy capital, hedge risk, and seize opportunities faster than any human trader could ever dream.

The difference between those who profit and those who get left behind will be simple: understanding this semantic layer now, before it becomes the invisible operating system of the new internet.

SECRET #6: AI's Role in the 2028 Wealth Explosion

Artificial Intelligence: The Web 3.0 Accelerator

If the Semantic Web is the **brain** of Web 3.0, then Artificial Intelligence is its **nervous system** processing signals, making decisions, and triggering actions in real time.

Thanks to breakthroughs in computing power, big data, and model architecture, AI is no longer a lab curiosity it's embedded in everyday life. From image recognition and voice assistants to personalized recommendations and real-time translations, AI already shapes how we interact with technology. The release of **ChatGPT-5** proved just how fast this is moving. GPT-5 isn't just a chatbot, it's a reasoning machine that can synthesize complex information, adapt to context, and deliver insights that feel like talking to a domain expert in any field.

In the Web 3.0 landscape, where oceans of data pour in daily from connected devices, decentralized apps, and blockchain transactions, AI is the force that can turn that data into action. Closed-loop workflows perception, decision-making, behavior, and feedback will run autonomously, continuously refining themselves without human intervention.

The applications are vast: autonomous vehicles navigating without delay, healthcare systems detecting illness before symptoms appear, DeFi protocols rebalancing portfolios in milliseconds, and smart cities that self-adjust traffic, power usage, and public safety in real time.

The 2028 AI–DeFi Convergence

By 2028, AI will be the command center for predictive DeFi protocols systems that don't just react to market conditions but anticipate them. Imagine a protocol that automatically scans thousands of blockchains, cross-references global economic indicators, analyzes social sentiment, and instantly reallocates assets to maximize returns or protect capital. No human team could move that fast, and no traditional institution could match the precision.

Those who understand this convergence now AI as the execution engine, DeFi as the value layer — will be positioned not just for good returns, but for **generational wealth**. The rest will be spectators, watching from the sidelines as autonomous systems create and capture value at a speed the old financial world simply can't match.

SECRET #7: Blockchain's Evolution Into Unstoppable Money

Blockchain Technology: Beyond Bitcoin

If AI is the execution engine of Web 3.0, blockchain is the **bedrock** the immutable ledger that turns every transaction into a permanent, verifiable truth. It's the technology that removes the need for trust by making fraud mathematically impossible and censorship prohibitively expensive.

While the idea of blockchain began forming in the cryptography circles of the 1980s and 1990s, it wasn't until 2008 with the release of Bitcoin's whitepaper that the world saw its first fully functional implementation. What followed was a global realization: money, records, and agreements could be managed without banks, governments, or corporate intermediaries.

Ethereum took this step further, introducing a **Turing-complete programming language** for smart contracts self-executing agreements written in code and decentralized applications (DApps) that run exactly as programmed. Its **Ethereum Virtual Machine (EVM)** acts as a sandbox, shielding contracts from malicious interference while enabling complex automation of financial systems, governance models, and digital economies.

From token systems and decentralized identity frameworks to decentralized autonomous organizations (DAOs) and blockchain-based file storage, the technology has spawned an ecosystem capable of rivaling and potentially replacing much of Big Tech's current monopoly on digital infrastructure.

And the next phase? **Semantic blockchain** and **knowledge-based blockchain** combining the transparency and security of blockchain with the contextual reasoning of artificial intelligence. Imagine a ledger that doesn't just record transactions, but understands them, predicts implications, and self-optimizes to protect value.

By 2028, blockchain won't just be "unstoppable money" it will be the operating system for decentralized finance, commerce, governance, and even AI-driven decision-making. Those who understand its trajectory now will see it not merely as a payment layer, but as the **foundation for the new digital economy.**

SECRET #8: The Storage Revolution That Breaks Big Tech

Decentralized Storage: Your Data, Your Control

If blockchain is the ledger of Web 3.0, decentralized storage is its **vault** the secure repository that ensures your data remains yours and cannot be quietly locked away, altered, or sold without your permission.

In the Web 2.0 era, there's been an unspoken deal: you hand over your data, and in return, you get "free" services. Your photos, your documents, your messages all stored on corporate servers, controlled by terms you didn't write, and siloed inside "data islands" that make migration or sharing difficult. In this setup, Big Tech holds the keys, and you're just a renter.

Decentralized storage changes the equation. By spreading encrypted fragments of your files across a peer-to-peer network, it eliminates single points of failure, censorship choke points, and the silent data mining that powers today's surveillance economy. Even if one node fails, the data lives on elsewhere and only you can unlock it.

Notable technologies are already leading the way:

- **IPFS (Inter-Planetary File System)** A peer-to-peer distributed file system designed to replace HTTP. It breaks files into small "blobs," assigns each a unique hash fingerprint, and records them in a distributed hash table. This makes content censorship-resistant and tamper-proof.

- **Filecoin & Arweave** These build on IPFS by adding incentive layers, rewarding network participants with tokens for providing storage and bandwidth. Filecoin operates like a decentralized marketplace for storage, while Arweave focuses on "permanent storage," preserving data indefinitely.

By 2028, decentralized storage will be the silent backbone of Web 3.0's most valuable systems from DeFi smart contracts storing mission-critical records to AI models keeping their training data secure, to entire metaverse worlds stored off centralized servers. Those who understand and invest in these infrastructure layers early won't just own digital assets they'll own the very spaces where the future's most valuable information lives.

SECRET #9: Edge Computing's Speed Advantage

Processing Power Where You Need It Most

In the race to dominate Web 3.0, speed isn't just a luxury its survival. The COVID-19 pandemic forced more of our lives online, and by 2020, global data volume had already exploded to **59 zettabytes**. That tidal wave of information overwhelmed traditional network infrastructure, revealing the bottlenecks of centralized cloud processing.

Edge computing flips the script. Instead of sending all your data to distant cloud servers for processing, it moves computing, storage, and decision-making **closer to the devices that generate the data** your phone, your **IoT device**, your local **node**. The result? Lightning-fast processing, reduced latency, and far lower bandwidth costs.

This **proximity** to the data source offers a decisive advantage:

- **Instant Analysis** Critical for real-time DeFi transactions where milliseconds can mean the difference between a gain and a loss.
- **Lower Energy Use** Processing locally avoids the power drain of constant long-distance data transfers.
- **Cost Efficiency** Less Bandwidth means less overhead for both users and decentralized

networks.

And here's where it gets even more powerful: integrating **Edge Computing** with **Federated Learning (FL)**. This combination allows AI models to train across multiple devices **without exposing raw data** meaning your node can contribute to global intelligence while keeping your private information locked down.

By 2028, DeFi protocols will run not just on blockchains but on a global mesh of edge devices, each making split-second decisions without waiting for a central authority. This will create an internet economy where transactions execute instantly, arbitrage opportunities are seized in real time, and latency becomes a relic of the Web 2.0 era. Those positioned at the edge literally will have the fastest access to the future's most lucrative opportunities.

SECRET #10: Cryptocurrencies and Tokens - The New Asset Class

Digital Assets That Will Define Wealth in 2028

If DeFi is the financial system of Web 3.0 and blockchain is its ledger, then **cryptocurrencies**

and tokens are the currency in your pocket the liquid assets that make this entire decentralized economy move.

In Web 3.0, cryptocurrencies aren't just speculative plays or "internet money." They are programmable assets that act as **mediums of exchange**, **stores of value**, and **units of account** across borderless, permissionless networks. Secured by cryptography and validated by decentralized consensus, they strip away the need for banks or clearing houses, letting value flow directly from person to person, anywhere on Earth.

Tokens extend this idea beyond money. Issued on blockchain networks, they represent ownership, access, or rights within a given ecosystem. Some unlock features in a decentralized application (DApp). Others represent fractional ownership in physical or digital assets. Some even function as voting power in decentralized governance systems.

In Web 3.0, two major types of tokens dominate:

1. **Utility Tokens:** These grant access to services or features within a

decentralized platform. Want storage on IPFS, a domain on ENS, or a subscription to a decentralized content network? You'll need the utility-token to get in.

2. **Protocol Tokens:** These are the native tokens of blockchain networks themselves. They incentivize participants to validate transactions, secure the network, and make governance decisions. Holding them often means having a voice in how the protocol evolves and a stake in its long-term success.

By 2028, this won't be a niche market it will be a **core asset class** alongside stocks, bonds, and real estate. Except unlike traditional markets, crypto assets trade 24/7, settle in minutes, and operate on open infrastructure that anyone can access. For those positioned early, the returns won't just come from holding coins they'll come from staking, governance, yield farming, and participating in ecosystems where tokens are the lifeblood of growth.

IPv6 Wealth Layer Model: From Clearnet to Sovereign Stack

It's not every day you stumble across a paradigm shift. But when you've spent enough time in the decentralized trenches building networks, testing protocols, and watching the crypto markets evolve your mind starts making connections. One day, while deep in network design, I found myself staring at the OSI model and the TCP/IP stack, and I asked myself: *What if?*

In the traditional internet world, the OSI and TCP/IP models formed the backbone of how data traveled from point A to point B. But in the decentralized future we're building where identity, data, and money flow peer-to-peer we need a different kind of stack. One that's not just about **information transfer**, but about **sovereign value circulation**.

That's where the **IPv6 Wealth Layer Model** comes in. It's a layered approach to Web 3.0 infrastructure that merges encrypted mesh networking, global IPv6 addressability, decentralized applications, and integrated financial logic into a full-cycle wealth engine.

IPv6 Wealth Layer Model (User)

Layer 1 - Clearnet User
Entry point from the traditional IPv4-based internet into the sovereign network. This is where the average user connects before crossing into the decentralized infrastructure.

Layer 2 - Gateway
An IPv4 NAT + Domain Proxy that bridges legacy systems with the sovereign IPv6 network, ensuring compatibility while maintaining control of the transition point.

Layer 3 - Bridge Layer
Handles Stablecoins, authentication protocols, and firewall logi acting as the financial and security handshake between networks.

Layer 4 - Corporate IPv6 Sovereign Network
Custom IPv6 subnets designed for organizational control, security, and privacy. This is the governance backbone for enterprise or community-scale deployment.

Layer 5 - Application Layer
Where decentralized apps live. Includes self-hosted infrastructure like Start9 servers, Ghost CMS, BTCPay Server for payments, and IPFS for content storage and distribution.

Layer 6 - Mesh Identity & Routing
CJDNS-powered node-based routing and trustless identity layer, ensuring encrypted, direct, and censorship-resistant communication across the network.

Layer 7 - Feedback Loop
The reinvestment layer. Systems like Satoshi for Storage, Data Vaults, and other decentralized revenue engines feed value back into the network, creating a self-sustaining economy.

Comprehensive Infrastructure View: The Sovereign Web Stack

The **IPv6 Wealth Layer Model** outlines the philosophy of building a value-first internet stack. The **Infrastructure Layers** are its boots-on-the-ground implementation of the actual tech stack you deploy to make the sovereign web real.

Here's how the pieces fit together:

Sovereign Stack Breakdown (Infrastructure View)

Infra 1 - Mesh & Identity Layer

Powered by CJDNS and Hyperboria, devices use cryptographic IPv6 addresses for decentralized routing and trustless identity. Every node is its own passport — encrypted, verifiable, and independent from centralized authorities.

Infra 2 - Sovereign Network Layer

An IPv6-native internal communications framework with stateless configuration, no NAT, and global addressability. This layer ensures devices and services can communicate securely without legacy internet bottlenecks.

Infra 3 - Application Layer

Self-hosted apps and services run here. This is where local infrastructure like Start9 servers, BTCPay Server, Ghost

CMS, Filebase, and IPFS gateways provide decentralized publishing, commerce, payments, and file storage without relying on Big Tech cloud platforms.

Infra 4 - Bridging Layer

Acts as the bilingual translator between the sovereign web and the legacy internet. Interfaces with IPv4 NAT, supports stablecoins, and connects to payment on-ramps like Strike, Coinbase, and Cash App. This is how users transition smoothly without friction.

Infra 5 - Value Transfer Layer

Handles money movement at internet speed. Uses Lightning Network, Ethereum Layer 2s, LNURL, and LNBits for real-time, low-cost payments across the globe. This layer turns the network into a functioning economic engine.

Infra 6 - Feedback Loop

The sustainability engine. Revenue from services like Satoshi For Storage is reinvested into mesh infrastructure, node expansion, and new decentralized applications. Every transaction strengthens the network's capacity and independence.

Together, these six infrastructure layers create more than just a network they create a **self-sustaining digital economy**. It's a closed loop: connect, build, transact, reinvest, and grow.

By 2028, networks running this architecture won't just participate in the new internet they'll own it, from the routing tables to the revenue streams.

Real-World Flow

A user uploads a file via Ghost CMS running on Start9. The request is routed over CJDNS, payment is made instantly over Lightning, and if needed, bridged to legacy rails via NAT or Strike. Logs are recorded, payments are auditable, and the revenue cycles back into infrastructure growth. The loop repeats — each pass making the network faster, stronger, and more sovereign.

Why This Matters

This model decentralizes identity, hosting, communication, and value transfer. It allows individuals and businesses to not just *use* the internet but own the rails it runs on. The result is a regenerative digital economy where the infrastructure itself grows in capacity and resilience with every transaction.

You're not just building apps - you're designing sovereignty.

Reclaiming the Network: CJDNS, Hyperboria, and the Bit Main Street Movement

Welcome visionary builders,

After building Bit Main Street and feeling the gravity of hosting a network bold enough to challenge the systems dominating today's digital landscape, a sobering realization crept in. It's the one that always walks in quietly right after the intoxicating ether fumes of optimism fade.

What's the purpose of building something revolutionary and sovereign... if they can just shut it down and throw me in jail like Ross Ulbricht?

We need a new way a digital sanctuary where honest, courageous entrepreneurs can build sovereign wealth without state interference. That's when I found something that changed everything: the Hyperboria privacy-friendly network.

Back in 2016, I was already toe deep into Ethereum, imagining how I could place Bit Main Street on the blockchain where no one could erase it as long as a node remained alive. I was searching for permanence, for freedom, and for a future that couldn't be seized.

Then I discovered Caleb James DeLisle and the concept of a mesh network a self -sustaining network of devices using IPv6 to communicate peer-to-peer, encrypted by default, without the middlemen. That's when I knew: **this was the path forward.**

What is CJDNS and Why Does It Matter to Us?

CJDNS the Caleb James DeLisle Network Suite is more than just a protocol. It's a revolutionary tool for building our own encrypted, decentralized internet. It gives every device a unique IPv6 address tied to a public key, so no central authority needs to assign us anything.

That means encryption is built-in, privacy is default, and we don't have to ask permission to connect.

Caleb James DeLisle, the mind behind CJDNS, is a developer and cryptography advocate who saw the cracks in the old internet long before it became fashionable to talk about decentralization. Frustrated by the way IPv4 and corporate ISPs centralized control, Caleb envisioned a network where encryption wasn't bolted on after the fact it was baked into the DNA. His work gave birth to CJDNS, a peer-to-peer IPv6 mesh networking protocol that could connect people directly, without going through the corporate chokepoints of the Clearnet.

From that vision, the community built Hyperboria, a global, encrypted mesh network that runs on CJDNS. Think of it as the "alternative internet" a parallel space where you can host your own services, run your own sites, and bypass the bottlenecks of traditional infrastructure. On Hyperboria, you can spin up your own YunoHost server to host email, websites, chat services, and file storage all under your control, on hardware you own, connected by a network that no ISP or government can quietly unplug. Hyperboria isn't just a tech experiment; it's a working, breathing example of what happens when people decide to stop renting digital space and start building their own.

CJDNS vs. Traditional Internet (IPv4 Clearnet):
Why the Mesh Wins

When you compare CJDNS mesh networking to the traditional IPv4 Clearnet, the differences aren't just technical, they're ideological. The Clearnet is built on control, surveillance, and gatekeeping. CJDNS is built on sovereignty, privacy, and community. Here's how they stack up.

IP Assignment By

On the Clearnet, your IP address is handed to you by an ISP a central authority that ultimately decides if and how you connect. In CJDNS, you generate your own IP address based on your cryptographic keys. That means you own it. No middleman, no permission slip.

Encryption

Clearnet encryption is optional. You might get it through HTTPS or a VPN, but it's an afterthought. CJDNS bakes encryption in from the start, giving you end-to-end protection by default.

NAT and Firewall Headaches

Port forwarding, double NAT, and firewall gymnastics are everyday frustrations on the Clearnet. With CJDNS, there's no NAT at all you get direct Routing between nodes, making connections smoother and faster.

Decentralization

Clearnet is governed by ISPs, tech giants, and governments. CJDNS flips the model: it's peer-to-peer and community controlled, meaning no single entity can dictate the rules.

Privacy

On the Clearnet, your ISP can log and monitor everything you do. In CJDNS, there are no logs and no central control, making mass surveillance a thing of the past.

Censorship Resistance

Clearnet sites can be blocked, filtered, or throttled with ease. On CJDNS, censorship is almost impossible without shutting down the nodes themselves — a far harder task in a distributed mesh.

DNS Dependency

Clearnet domains depend on centralized DNS servers like Google or Cloudflare. CJDNS uses its own. CJD addresses built directly into the mesh, removing that point of failure.

IP Traceability

On the Clearnet, your IP is tied to your location and ISP account, making you easy to track. In CJDNS, your IP is your cryptographic identity, revealing nothing about your physical location.

Interconnectivity

The Clearnet relies on centralized peering agreements between ISPs. CJDNS nodes link autonomously, without ISP mediation, creating a truly free-flowing network.

Network Growth

Clearnet expansion happens top-down new nodes and infrastructure are added only when ISPs decide. CJDNS grows bottom-up anyone can join by peering, fueling organic, unstoppable growth.

If you're building for Web 3.0 and beyond, understanding this shift is essential. CJDNS isn't just another networking protocol, it's the foundation for a sovereign internet economy. It's what lets Bit Main Street, and any future decentralized marketplace exist without bending the knee to centralized gatekeepers.

Why It Matters to the Bit Main Street Community

We're not here just to build websites. We're here to build **digital sovereignty** - the freedom to create, speak, trade, and educate *without corporate gatekeepers or surveillance*.

With CJDNS, Hyperboria, and Yggdrasil working in unison, we can:

- **Run our own mesh-powered marketplace,** one that no ISP or government can shut down.

- **Host encrypted, peer-to-peer learning spaces** for DeFi Jedi Masterclasses and digital empowerment programs.
- **Operate our own private communication tools** chat, video, voice all running inside the mesh.
- **Turn homes and local hubs into access points**, expanding the network without depending on AT&T, Comcast, or big tech.

This isn't just tech, this is **laying down fiber in the mind**: a secure, resilient network owned by us, for us.

This Ain't Just Networking Its Liberation

The old internet, IPv4, was designed for military control and corporate profit. What we're doing with CJDNS and Hyperboria is flipping that script. We're decentralizing power. We're reclaiming our digital land. The Clearnet is the plantation.

Hyperboria is an underground railroad. And networks like Bit Main Street? That's the train station -where you board the encrypted express heading straight into the future.

And here's the part they don't tell you: you don't have to just be a passenger. If you decide to build your own network, you can connect directly with Bit Main Street. The moment you do, our communication model expands not in theory, but in practice. Your node strengthens the route, your community becomes a stop on the line, and your data flows with the same privacy, security, and sovereignty that fuels our own. This isn't just technology, it's infrastructure you own, connections you control, and a future you help shape.

Let's plug in. Let's peer up. Let's build the MESH a living, breathing network of freedom that grows stronger with every connection.

Want to stay connected and learn how we're building this decentralized future?

Join the Bit Main Street Market Newsletter where we share tools, strategies, and behind-the-scenes insights to help you thrive in Web 3.0.

Yggdrasil's End-to-End Encrypted IPv6 Mesh Networking

As we imagine the future of Web 3.0, one name emerged during research that felt ancient, symbolic, and powerful all at once: **Yggdrasil**.

In Norse mythology, Yggdrasil was the sacred ash tree whose roots reached across distant worlds, and whose branches touched the heavens. It was a connector of realms, a living bridge between what was, what is, and what could be. That same energy is reborn today through a protocol bearing its name: a real-world network architecture designed to unify people and systems without centralized control.

Technically speaking, **Yggdrasil is an open-source, self-configuring mesh network built on end-to-end encrypted IPv6**. It enables any node, anywhere in the world, to connect securely without needing traditional IP assignment, VPNs, or ISPs. In short, it's a network that builds itself, heals itself, and protects itself by design.

It's like the *Tree of Souls* from *Avatar*, hidden deep in the Hallelujah Mountains. But instead of just connecting consciousness, this one connects devices, communities, and purpose **securely and peer-to-peer**.

Now imagine **Bit Main Street Network**:

- Small Raspberry Pi nodes running Yggdrasil or CJDNS.
- Hosting content and marketplaces.
- Running Bitcoin Lightning services.
- Acting as the living backbone of **sovereign digital economies**.

This isn't science fiction it's the architecture of a future where **we own the pipes, the platforms, and the profits**.

IDEA - Freedom Movie Theater

A Vision You Can Build Today

Imagine this: a cozy meet-up space, maybe your favorite local bar, buzzing with conversation. A projector casts a film onto the wall, but this isn't Netflix, Hulu, or Amazon Prime.

This is your stream.

Sovereign. Self-hosted. Running on a mesh of local nodes. **Think Teleparty**, but without surveillance, without gatekeepers, and without corporate choke points.

Just community, content, and encrypted connections all on real Web 3.0 infrastructure.

How It Works (The Build Blueprint)

1. Local Mesh Streaming Setup

Set up a local IPv6 mesh network powered by Yggdrasil or CJDNS.

Pre - cache the movie using IPFS or torrents.

Optionally stream live from a lead node using WebRTC for real-time events.

2. Smart Nodes as Media Servers

Deploy Raspberry Pi 4 or 5 units as lightweight media hubs.

Use one anchor node as the main seeder for the film.

Store content on external SSDs for faster read/write and HD/4K compatibility.

3. Decentralized Identity & Access Control

Assign encrypted mesh identities to attendees.

Gate entry via Lightning micropayments or a local whitelist.

Sell access tokens as collectibles for repeat events.

4. Playback Sync

Use WebRTC timestamps + CRDTs for exact frame alignment.

Keep every screen in sync — whether it's the big projector or a phone in the back row.

Challenges & Solutions

» **Bandwidth:** Raspberry Pi can choke on 4K pair them with SSDs or a mini-PC seed box
» **Mesh Stability:** If a node drops, playback can glitch use offline-first caching and fallback streams.
» **Sync Precision:** No central clock. Use timestamp offsets in WebRTC to maintain perfect sync.
» **Scaling Across Cities:** Keep each venue self-contained, then federate them with optional relays.
» **Access Restrictions:** Pair mesh identities with Lightning paywalls to control guest

access.

Real-World Stack Example

» **Media:** Hosted via IPFS or local SSD, served through a local web server
» **Network:** Encrypted IPv6 via Yggdrasil or CJDNS
» **Front-end:** React-based viewing app, optionally cast to a screen
» **Access Control:** Lightning-based micropayments or mesh credentials
» **Sync:** WebRTC and CRDTs for real-time frame sync

Why It Matters

As AI continues to reshape the global job market, we must plant new seeds systems that let people **create**, **connect**, and **earn** outside of traditional tech monopolies. This isn't just about media. It's about ownership. It's about building public squares and creative spaces for the Web 3.0 generation.

Yggdrasil and mesh networks like it aren't science fiction they're here now. And the time to build with them is today.

Let the Freedom Movie Theater be your symbol.

Let Bit Main Street be your blueprint.

Let decentralization be your path forward.

Web 3.0: The Game Changer for 2028 Wealth Creation

The concept of Web 3.0 has been subject to ongoing interpretations with shifting paradigms. From its roots in the semantic web to the current manifestation as a decentralized network, the vision of Web 3.0 has evolved over time. With each iteration, the Internet of Everything becomes more intelligent, three-dimensional, and decentralized, emerging as defining characteristics of the Web 3.0 landscape.

However, the promise of decentralization also brings challenges. While empowering users, decentralization complicates regulatory efforts, particularly in addressing issues like hate speech, violence, and terrorism. Moreover, the development of Web 3.0 is still in its nascent stages, with ongoing technological innovation and implementation processes accompanied by associated risks.

As a result, it appears that Web 2.0 and Web 3.0 will coexist for the foreseeable future, each contributing to the evolving digital landscape in its own way. Understanding this technological foundation becomes crucial for recognizing which protocols will survive and thrive in the coming transformation.

The next chapter reveals the shocking truth about how this technological resilience played out during the greatest crypto crisis in history, and why those who understood these foundations were the only ones who saw it coming.

Chapter 3

Unlocking the Secrets - The Great Deception Unveiled

"And also, that nation, whom they shall serve, will I judge: and afterward shall they come out with great substance."

How the Illusion of Freedom Was Engineered, and the Web 3.0 Blueprint That Breaks It

Promises of Freedom

At first, the internet brought us a new sense of freedom. When it first came out for the general public, people were delighted. It was envisioned as a tool to democratize knowledge, foster global collaboration, and facilitate communication with anyone, anywhere.

If you were to answer about the promises of freedom without looking up, you'd likely say that being free means being able to act, speak, or think as you wish without any external influence. This is a common belief, even though such absolute freedom doesn't and can't exist in reality.

Why is that? While the idea of acting without consequences might sound appealing, it overlooks the complexities of real life. We live in a society that constantly interacts with others who should also enjoy the same freedoms. Absolute freedom would lead to chaos, as without rules, anyone could commit murder, steal, profane, or completely disregard others, all in the name of freedom.

For freedom to be as equal for everyone as possible, we need some rules to govern it. Throughout history, societies have organized in various ways to live out their own versions of freedom. While we have not reached a consensus on what true freedom is, we now at least have the possibility to discuss it within certain boundaries.

Thus, attainable (real) freedom requires certain limits to exist. We accept that there are criminal laws (and their subsequent punishments) for actions deemed as crimes. We renounce a part of our freedom (e.g., agreeing not to steal) to ensure another type of freedom that serves what we perceive as a higher purpose.

With this in mind and a somewhat clearer idea of what freedom might look like, we can now analyze how technology impacts and reshapes that concept.

When it first aired in 2011, the science fiction anthology series *Black Mirror* resonated deeply, particularly with younger generations. Why? Through its fictionalized stories, the series invited us to examine the darker side of technology. The episode *Nosedive* portrayed a world where people rated each interaction on a one-to-five-star scale, directly affecting socioeconomic status.

While this might seem far-fetched, the existence of credit scores in China should make us feel at least a little uneasy. Could we really live in a world like that? Technology is advancing at breakneck speed, yet very few are pausing to consider whether the direction we are headed is the right path to take.

Data lies at the heart of this dilemma. We now have access to the largest amount of data in history. With the help of artificial intelligence (AI), we can sift through these vast troves of information to uncover actionable insights. But we are also living in extremely dangerous times.

Around the same time Bitcoin came on the scene, I began delving deeply into the economic system. By 2013, the idea of creating Bit Main Street came to me. Two years later, Ethereum and Smart Contracts emerged, offering a solution to Bitcoin's latency problem. Fast-forward to today, blockchain plus Smart

Contracts can support mortgages, insurance, pensions, and much more.

This is why I believe Web 3.0 offers a realistic solution to our current problems. CBDCs are the antithesis of this vision. The Bitcoin vs. "Shitcoin" debate is a distraction. The focus should be on integration, interoperability, and fulfilling Satoshi Nakamoto's vision while making the network unstoppable.

Promises of Web 3.0 - The Stakes Are Now Higher

The internet's evolution has been extraordinary, moving from static pages (Web 1.0) to the dynamic platforms of Web 2.0. But now, Web 3.0 stands as the fork in the road - and the choice is stark: decentralization or **digital feudalism**.

At the heart of Web 3.0 is **decentralization**, which removes intermediaries and gives individuals direct peer-to-peer control. In Web 2.0, platforms, banks, and big tech decide what you can say, buy, or store. In Web 3.0, the power shifts back to the user.

Privacy is the second pillar. Today, data is the oil of the 21st century, and you're the oil well. In Web 3.0, technologies like **zero-knowledge proofs** and decentralized storage make it possible to transact, share, and collaborate without exposing sensitive information.

Ownership is the third pillar. In Web 3.0, you *own* your data, your assets, and your identity. Smart contracts enforce this ownership automatically, without needing a lawyer or corporate middleman.

But here's the warning shot: Central Bank Digital Currencies (CBDCs) are still coming, and they are not "crypto" in the freedom sense. Even though the U.S. Genius Act and similar measures in other nations have, for now, halted official CBDC launches and left the door open for certain regulated stablecoins, that pause is temporary. Across the globe from the EU to Africa to Asia governments are experimenting, legislating, and preparing the infrastructure to roll out programmable money.

And programmable money is not neutral. CBDCs are money with a kill switch. Governments could restrict purchases, freeze accounts, or enforce negative interest rates all automatically, all without due process.

If Web 3.0 is the open sea, CBDCs are the walled aquarium. The fish are still alive but only as long as the keeper allows.

This is not just America's problem it's a warning for the world. Whether you live under a democracy, a monarchy, or a one-party state, the danger is the same: CBDCs consolidate financial power in the hands of a few, and that power can and will be used to control the many.

The Call to Action: We must integrate Web 3.0 tools now not tomorrow to build a decentralized, private, and user-controlled economy before CBDCs lock humanity into permanent surveillance finance.

The Perfect Storm That Changed Everything

After the curious implosion of FTX, the crypto market became gripped with fear and stagnation. Meanwhile, the poster child for capitalism was exposed as economic freedom for the everyday American citizen vanished, as the disillusion of artificial freedom rapidly faded into recent memory. But for those who understood the deeper game being played and the technological foundations we explored in the previous chapters, hope emerged in the form of decentralized digital currency.

This is the story of how we unlock the secrets of decentralized finance to guide us out of that orchestrated chaos.

The script was almost too perfect to be coincidental. In 2021, after the first year of pandemic lockdowns sent the global economy into a downward spiral, a miracle happened. The promise of Bitcoin and DeFi became reality as the second wave of alternative currencies brought hope. NFTs exploded, Bitcoin climbed to nearly $70,000, and the roaring twenties seemed here again. The crypto winter was over, the Bitcoin halving had arrived, and Web 3.0 technology proved how blockchain could fix the problems of the antiquated fiat system.

Sadly, the euphoria was short-lived.

Like a script from a Hollywood movie, the most popular, well-connected political crypto exchange to ever exist imploded. FTX worth $32 billion in cryptocurrency just weeks earlier went bankrupt overnight, taking market momentum with it. The crypto market became the primary target of the SEC, while the agency conveniently ignored its close ties to the FTX players. As media coverage intensified, the similarities between Bernie Madoff and Sam Bankman-Fried became undeniable. The SEC finally had its excuse to curtail freedoms for everyday American citizens through what we might call "Crypto 911."

And just in time, on the heels of Fed Coin and global Central Bank Digital Currency initiatives, FTX imploded. One year later, paper Bitcoin was born in the form of ETFs as BlackRock became the largest controller of the funds. Is anyone else seeing this pattern?

If you do, then please read on because the secrets I'm about to reveal will change everything you thought you knew about this orchestrated chaos.

SECRET #11: The Protocols That Never Broke

The Technical Reality Behind the Theater

Here's the first secret most people missed: True DeFi protocols never stopped working during the FTX collapse. While centralized exchanges crumbled, decentralized protocols like Uniswap, Aava, and MakerDAO continued operating flawlessly.

The infrastructure that actually matters the smart contracts, the liquidity pools, the governance mechanisms remained intact and functional.

This wasn't luck. It was design.

The Architecture of Resilience

No Central Point of Failure: Unlike FTX's centralized order books and custody systems, DeFi protocols operate through immutable smart contracts distributed across thousands of nodes

Transparent Reserves: Every token in a DeFi protocol is verifiable on-chain, unlike the phantom reserves that brought down FTX

Permissionless Operation: No CEO can make backroom deals with user funds when the protocol itself controls the treasury through coded logic

During the FTX collapse, while centralized platforms froze withdrawals and filed for bankruptcy, DeFi users continued swapping tokens, earning yields, and maintaining full custody of their assets.

The contrast couldn't have been starker — or more revealing.

SECRET #12: The 2025 Regulatory Revolution

The Great Reversal

The second secret? The 2025 regulatory landscape represents the most significant shift toward DeFi adoption in history. The very protocols that survived the FTX winter are now being recognized as the solution, not the problem.

Three Revolutionary Bills That Changed Everything

In just one month, Congress passed three groundbreaking crypto bills that fundamentally transformed the American regulatory landscape:

GENIUS Act – Stablecoin Regulation (Signed July 18, 2025)

Official Bill: S. 1582 – "Guiding and Establishing National Innovation for U.S. Stablecoins Act"

What it does:

Establishes the first federal framework for stablecoins

Requires 1:1 backing with U.S. dollars or low-risk assets

Mandates monthly audits & proof of reserves, plus AML and consumer protections

Creates a dual oversight regime between federal and state supervisors

Timeline:

Passed Senate 68–30 on June 17, 2025

Passed House 308–122 on July 17, 2025

Signed into law by President Trump on July 18, 2025

Benefits vs. Gensler era: Pre-GENIUS, Stablecoins were largely unregulated, often using fractional reserves. Gensler's SEC focused on enforcement rather than clear rule-making. Now, stablecoin issuers have clear legal guardrails, spurring institutional interest and bolstering consumer confidence.

CLARITY Act – Crypto Market Structure (House Passed July 17, 2025)

Official Bill: H.R. 3633 – Digital Asset Market Clarity Act of 2025

What it does:

Defines criteria distinguishing securities (SEC) vs commodities (CFTC)

Grants the CFTC primary authority over decentralized digital assets, while the SEC retains jurisdiction over securities and investment tokens

Offers safe-harbor provisions for token fundraising below $75 million threshold

Status: Passed House 294–134 on July 17, 2025. Now awaiting, Senate review.

Benefits vs. Gensler era: Under Gensler's SEC, regulation-by-enforcement was rampant (Ripple, Coinbase subpoenas), with limited clarity. This act replaces unpredictability with objective definitions, empowering projects and investors with legal certainty.

Anti-CBDC Act – Blocking Central Bank Digital Currency (Passed)

Official Bills: S. 1124 (Senate) / H.R. 1919 (House) – Anti-CBDC Surveillance State Act

What it does:

Prohibits the Federal Reserve from creating a retail CBDC

Passed via attached amendment (219–210) within the must-pass defense bill

Why it matters: Addresses privacy concerns around potential Fed surveillance via CBDCs and reflects broader ideological opposition to centralizing monetary power via digital means.

Benefits vs. Gensler era: While Gensler didn't actively support CBDCs, no legislative ban existed. The act cements a legal barrier, ensuring consumer privacy remains protected and federal digital currency cannot proceed unchecked.

THE IRS CAPITULATION

On April 10, 2025, President Trump signed legislation that nullified the digital asset reporting obligations imposed on DeFi brokers under Section 80603 of the Infrastructure Investment and Jobs Act. Combined with these three new bills, this represents the most comprehensive pro-crypto legislative package in American history.

Summary Comparison: Gensler Era vs. New Laws

Stablecoin regulations: From ad-hoc enforcement to GENIUS Act's 1:1 reserves, audits, and consumer protections

Asset classification: From SEC-driven enforcement to CLARITY Act's clear SEC/CFTC jurisdiction

CBDC development: From unregulated Fed discretion to explicit ban on retail Fed digital dollar

Regulatory predictability: From high uncertainty to enhanced transparency and investor confidence

Why This Matters: Innovation boost with lawful frameworks, consumer trust through mandatory audits, privacy preserved with no Fed-run digital currency, and market clarity where projects know upfront their regulatory status.

SECRET #13: The Uniswap Vindication

The Investigation That Revealed Everything

In February 2025, the SEC closed its investigation of Uniswap without any enforcement action, a stark departure from the treatment of centralized peers like Kraken and Binance. This wasn't mercy; it was recognition of a fundamental distinction.

The Decentralization Test

The Uniswap decision revealed the regulatory "decentralization test" that now separates legitimate DeFi protocols from centralized platforms masquerading as decentralized:

1. **Governance Decentralization:** True governance token distribution and decision-making processes
2. **Technical Decentralization:** Smart contracts that operate without administrative control
3. **Economic Decentralization:** Protocol revenue distributed to participants, not extracted by centralized entities

Protocols that pass this test now enjoy regulatory clarity that was unimaginable just two years ago.

SECRET #14: The Solution Hidden in Plain Sight

The Renaissance of Truth, Justice, and Freedom

If I were to tell you the solution to the orchestrated financial control system was already solved and functioning, how would you feel? If you said you'd feel good, then great—

keep feeling good, because the roaring twenties is still here. The idea is still alive and well.

The technologies I'm about to reveal have the potential to free humanity from the grasp of this dying fiat system and bring us into an era of financial sovereignty not seen since Reconstruction and the Black Wall Street Era.

THE CURRENT STATE OF TRUE DEFI

Despite media fear-mongering and regulatory uncertainty, the DeFi ecosystem has quietly achieved several breakthrough developments:

» **Institutional Integration:** Traditional financial institutions are now integrating DeFi protocols into their operations, recognizing their superior efficiency and transparency

» **Cross-Chain Maturation:** Interoperability solutions have become robust enough to support enterprise-level operations across multiple blockchain networks

» **Security Evolution:** Enhanced smart contract auditing standards and security practices have emerged, making DeFi protocols more secure than many traditional financial systems

» **Yield Optimization:** Advanced strategies

now exist that can generate sustainable returns while maintaining risk management principles that centralized systems cannot match

The Path Forward: Your Guide to Financial Sovereignty

During the crypto technology boom of 2021, I wrote *Tangible Economic Freedom with the Decentralized Financial Ecosystem.* It outlined how to set up DeFi wallets and linked to exchanges that were later banned from serving American citizens after the Sam Bankman-Fried Hollywood-style debacle.

The information was still relevant, but if you were American living in the land of the free and home of the brave, you were told you couldn't spend your money the way you wanted. The plan was to get you into Central Bank Digital Currency a system where you cannot buy or sell anything outside of what the owners of fiat tell you to.

If this sounds horrible to you, you are not alone.

The 2025 Revelation

But here's the secret they don't want you to know: the 2025 regulatory landscape has fundamentally changed the game. The protocols that survived the FTX winter now have unprecedented regulatory clarity and operational freedom. The tools for financial sovereignty are not only available; they're being officially recognized as legitimate financial infrastructure.

This book will unlock every secret you need to navigate this new landscape with confidence, technical competence, and regulatory compliance. You'll learn not just how to use DeFi protocols, but how to understand their fundamental architecture, assess their risks, and maximize their potential while staying completely within the bounds of current law.

The renaissance of financial freedom is here.

Let's unlock its secrets together.

Chapter 4

The Hidden Architecture - DeFi Fundamentals Revealed

"Explore the new frontier of finance with expert tips and real-world tactics to unlock digital wealth."

The Greatest Heist in History - And the Slap on the Wrist That Followed

Before we dive into the technical architecture that makes DeFi protocols unbreakable, let's examine the stunning contrast between centralized fraud and decentralized resilience. Caroline Ellison, former CEO of Alameda Research, was sentenced to just 24 months in prison for her role in stealing $8 billion in customer funds from FTX. Let that sink in: Two years for stealing $8 billion.

Judge Lewis Kaplan acknowledged this was potentially "the greatest financial fraud ever perpetrated in this country and probably anywhere else," yet the woman who helped orchestrate it will be free by July 2026. Meanwhile, Sam Bankman-Fried received 25 years, but even he faced a maximum of 110 years for crimes that destroyed thousands of lives and billions in savings.

The Real Scandal:

While Ellison serves her minimal sentence in a low-security Connecticut facility, something extraordinary was happening in the very system they tried to destroy.

The Rise of Digital Fascism

We're living through a digital arms race. On one side, we have tools for **privacy, decentralization, individual control** - encryption, blockchain, decentralized networks. On the other side, those same tools can be twisted into **weapons of control**.

- **Encryption**: A shield for privacy… or a cloak for mass surveillance.
- **Decentralized networks**: A path to distribute power… or a way for hidden actors to silently control global flows of information.
- **Smart devices & IoT**: They make life convenient… while vacuuming up data that could be weaponized against you.

In the wrong hands, **freedom tech becomes control tech**.

Is Digital Fascism Already Here?

Classic fascism had newspapers and radio. Digital fascism has **social feeds and algorithmic propaganda**.

It thrives in decentralized spaces that were supposed to empower individuals - using the same peer-to-peer structures to spread manipulation, fear, and political extremism. It dresses in memes, viral videos, and "alternative news" headlines, but underneath, the playbook hasn't changed since **Mussolini**:

- Create an eternal enemy.
- Stoke fear of an external threat.
- Demand loyalty to the nation or ideology above all else.

Globalization and real-time communication have made this more powerful than ever. You can now watch, influence, and mobilize people on another continent in seconds. And the darker players are doing exactly that.

Web 3.0 Security Risks You Can't Ignore

Let's get specific. Web 3.0 offers incredible opportunities for sovereignty but it's also a **battlefield**:

1. **Decentralized Vulnerabilities -** A 51% attack can compromise an entire blockchain if one entity gains enough control over nodes or validators.
2. **Surveillance Potential -** Malicious actors, including states, can still infiltrate networks and monitor activity.
3. **New Centralization Risks -** Power can re-accumulate in the hands of whales, mining cartels, or dominant staking providers.
4. **Misuse of Technology -** Smart contracts could enforce oppressive regulations or censorship just as easily as they enable trustless trade.
5. **CBDCs -** Programmable money with a kill switch. Governments could freeze your funds, limit purchases, or impose expiry dates on your money automatically.
6. **Scalability Bottlenecks -** Network congestion and high fees can drive people back to centralized alternatives, eroding decentralization.

The CBDC Warning Shot

CBDCs are coming and they're not "crypto" in the freedom sense.

The Genius Act and other legislation in the U.S. have slowed direct CBDC rollout for now, allowing stablecoins instead but this is just a pause, not a victory. Around the world, countries are already piloting and launching CBDCs.

If Web 3.0 is the open sea, CBDCs are the walled aquarium. The fish are still alive but only as long as the keeper allows.

The call to action: integrate Web 3.0 tools now not later to build decentralized, private, user-controlled economies before CBDCs lock us into permanent surveillance finance.

The Architecture of Freedom

DeFi has proven it can survive the collapse of giants. But it can't survive apathy.

The fight isn't just *centralized vs. decentralized* its sovereign finance vs. programmable compliance. And the battlefield isn't in the future, it's here, now.

And here's where the political script flips. The same political machine that once tried to crush crypto is now moving to embrace it. Is it a genuine shift... or a hostile takeover in disguise?

SECRET #15: The Trump Revolution - From Crypto Destroyer to Crypto Creator

Just two years ago, Gary Gensler, who was suspiciously connected to FTX through meetings with Sam Bankman-Fried and his MIT blockchain course connections, was systematically destroying cryptocurrency through SEC enforcement actions. The irony is staggering: Gensler had historically had ties to Bankman-Fried's father through their affiliation at MIT, and SEC documents confirm that Gensler met with Sam Bankman-Fried and two other FTX personnel in March, discussing "conditional no-action relief."

The Stunning Reversal: Fast forward to 2025, and the President of the United States has created his own cryptocurrency token TRUMP coin which launched at approximately $1.21 and skyrocketed to an all-time high of $75.35

within days, achieving a market capitalization exceeding $14.5 billion.

Think about this timeline:

- 2022-2023: Gensler destroys crypto through regulatory warfare
- 2024: FTX collapses, revealing deep regulatory capture
- 2025: Trump creates the most successful political meme coin in history

This isn't just market dynamics it's a complete paradigm shift that reveals the true power of decentralized protocols.

SECRET #16: The Smart Contract Conspiracy - Why DeFi Survived While FTX Died

The Architecture of Truth vs. The Architecture of Lies

While FTX operated on lies, hidden reserves, and backroom deals, DeFi protocols operate on mathematical certainty and transparent code. Here's the fundamental difference:

- **Liquidity Provision - The Unbreakable Engine:** Beyond simple token swaps, liquidity providers earn fees by depositing token pairs into automated market makers (AMMs). Unlike FTX's fake liquidity that disappeared overnight, DeFi liquidity is:

» **Verifiable on-chain:** Every token is accountable through blockchain verification

» **Non-custodial:** No single entity can steal or misappropriate funds

» **Mathematically governed:** Smart contracts execute trades without human intervention

Understanding impermanent loss, fee structures, and liquidity mining rewards is crucial for optimizing returns, but more importantly, these mechanisms create a system where theft is mathematically impossible.

- **Yield Farming - The Anti-Alameda Strategy:** Strategic deployment of capital across multiple DeFi protocols to maximize yields involves:

- **Composite yields and auto-compounding:** Unlike Alameda's gambling with customer funds, DeFi yields are transparent and verifiable

- **Token emission schedules:** Smart contracts control token distribution, preventing insider manipulation
- **Risk-adjusted returns:** Algorithms calculate risk without human bias or fraud
- **Opportunity costs:** Every trade is transparent and auditable
- **Flash Loans - The Ultimate Transparency Tool:** Uncollateralized loans that must be repaid within a single transaction. While powerful for arbitrage and refinancing, they require technical expertise and carry smart contract risks. But here's the secret: Flash loans make fraud impossible because every transaction must be completed within the same block, preventing the kind of long-term manipulation that destroyed FTX.

SECRET #17: Smart Contract Architecture - The Unbreakable Code

Modern DeFi protocols implement security patterns that make FTX-style fraud impossible:

- **Upgradeable Contracts:** Many protocols use proxy patterns to allow for bug fixes and feature additions while maintaining state. Understanding the governance mechanisms behind these upgrades is essential because:
- **Time locks prevent instant changes:** Unlike FTX's ability to instantly move funds, DeFi protocols require time delays for any modifications
- **Community governance:** Token holders vote on changes, preventing single-point-of-failure leadership
- **Transparent processes:** All proposed changes are visible to the entire community
- **Multi-Signature Wallets:** Critical functions often require multiple signatures, distributing control among team members or governance participants. This is the opposite of FTX's centralized control where

Bankman-Fried could unilaterally move billions.

- **Time Locks:** Important changes are often subject to time delays, allowing the community to review and potentially veto harmful modifications. This prevents the overnight fund transfers that destroyed FTX customers.

SECRET #18: The Risk Assessment Framework That Actually Works

Unlike the fake risk management at FTX, intermediate users should evaluate DeFi protocols across multiple dimensions:

Technical Risk Assessment:

- **Smart contract audit quality and recency:** Unlike FTX's unaudited code, legitimate DeFi protocols undergo multiple independent audits
- **Code complexity and testing coverage:** Open source code allows independent verification
- **Upgrade mechanisms and governance structure:** Transparent

processes   prevent   backdoor manipulations

Economic Risk Analysis:

- **Tokenomics and inflation schedules:** Mathematically defined, unlike FTX's arbitrary token printing
- **Liquidity depth and concentration:** Verifiable on-chain, preventing fake liquidity reports
- **Yield sustainability:** Calculated through transparent algorithms, not backroom deals

Operational Risk Management:

- **Team anonymity and track record:** While some teams are anonymous, their code is not
- **Centralization points:** Identifying and minimizing single points of failure
- **Regulatory compliance status:** Operating within the new 2025 regulatory framework

The Trump Factor: Political Legitimacy Meets Technical Excellence

TRUMP coin's meteoric rise from $1.21 to $75.35 in just days demonstrates something profound: when political legitimacy meets blockchain technology, the results are explosive. This isn't just about meme coins it's about the fundamental shift where:

- Political figures embrace crypto instead of destroying it
- Regulatory clarity enables innovation instead of stifling it
- Blockchain technology has achieved mainstream political acceptance

The Technical Lesson: While centralized platforms like FTX can be destroyed by a single bad actor, decentralized protocols continue operating regardless of external political or regulatory pressure. The Trump coin phenomenon proves that blockchain technology has achieved mainstream political acceptance, something that seemed impossible during the Gensler enforcement era.

The Path Forward: Technical Mastery in the New Era

Understanding these fundamentals isn't just about making money it's about participating in a financial revolution that has survived its greatest test. While Caroline Ellison serves her minimal sentence and Gary Gensler fades into regulatory history, the protocols that matter continue building the future of finance.

Next, we'll explore the current DeFi ecosystem and reveal which platforms have not only survived the FTX winter but emerged stronger and more valuable than ever before.

Chapter 5

The Underground Economy - Current DeFi Ecosystem Exposed

"Uncover the secrets of decentralized finance and take charge of your financial freedom today."

Welcome to the part of the book where the warnings turn into weapons. You've seen the traps, the scams, the politics, and the power plays. Now it's time to look under the hood of the real machine the protocols and platforms that didn't just survive the FTX winter, but came out sharper, stronger, and ready to rewrite the rules of money.

This is not Wall Street's economy. This is the underground network - alive, borderless, censorship-resistant where ideas move faster than laws, and innovation doesn't need permission.

If Chapter 4 was the warning, this is the map. We're about to pull back the curtain on the current DeFi ecosystem revealing the platforms that didn't just survive the FTX winter, but came out faster, stronger, and more valuable than ever before.

These aren't just investment opportunities. They are the infrastructure of the next financial era the tools you'll need to operate, profit, and protect your sovereignty in the years ahead.

SECRET #19: The Great Geographic Divide - Why Location Determines Your Financial Freedom

The Uncomfortable Truth About American Financial Restrictions

Here's a secret that will make your blood boil: Users outside the United States have significantly more financial freedom than Americans when it comes to DeFi. While the rest of the world enjoys unrestricted access to the most innovative financial protocols ever created, Americans have been systematically locked out by their own government's regulatory warfare.

But before you despair, here's the plot twist: things are finally looking up.

President Trump signed legislation on April 10, 2025, that nullified the digital asset reporting obligations imposed on decentralized finance (DeFi) brokers under Section 80603 of the Infrastructure Investment and Jobs Act. This represents the most significant reversal of anti-crypto legislation in American history.

The Power of New Laws Reversed:

The legislation, which passed with bipartisan support, specifically exempts DeFi brokers that operate almost entirely on blockchain infrastructure from:

- Form 1099-DA reporting requirements
- Know Your Customer (KYC) information collection
- Transaction data reporting to the IRS

What This Means for Americans:

- True DeFi protocols are now exempt from burdensome reporting
- Permissionless blockchain protocols can operate without surveillance
- Innovation can flourish without compliance nightmares

However, the Geographic Reality Remains: While progress is being made, Americans still face restrictions that users in Switzerland, Singapore, or the UAE simply don't encounter. International users can access every major DeFi platform without geographic restrictions, VPN requirements, or regulatory uncertainty.

SECRET #20: The Leading Lending Platforms and Who Can Actually Use Them

Aave (AAVE) - The Swiss Army Knife of DeFi Lending

Website: https://aave.com/

US Status: Fully accessible to Americans as of 2025

Key Features: Flash loans, credit delegation, yield farming

Security: Multiple audits, bug bounty program, never hacked during FTX chaos

Governance: Decentralized governance with AAVE token

International Advantage: Global users can access all features without restrictions

The Secret: Aave's flash loan feature allows anyone to borrow millions of dollars without collateral, as long as the loan is repaid within the same transaction. This is impossible in traditional finance and showcases DeFi's true revolutionary potential.

Compound (COMP) - The Pioneer That Changed Everything

Website: https://compound.finance/

US Status: Accessible with recent regulatory clarity

Key Features: Algorithmic interest rates, cToken system

Innovation: Pioneered DeFi lending protocols, spawning entire industry

Integration: Widely integrated across DeFi ecosystem

Global Access: Unrestricted international usage

The Secret: Compound's algorithmic interest rate model automatically adjusts rates based on supply and demand, creating a more efficient lending market than any bank could offer.

MakerDAO (MKR) - The Stablecoin Empire

Website: https://makerdao.com/

US Status: Fully operational for Americans

Key Features: DAI stablecoin, collateralized debt positions

Governance: Mature decentralized governance system

Stability: Proven resilience through market cycles, including FTX collapse

International Freedom: Global users enjoy unrestricted access to all vaults

The Secret: MakerDAO's DAI stablecoin maintains its $1 peg through algorithmic governance, not central bank manipulation. It's proof that decentralized systems can create more stable money than governments.

Emerging Platforms Gaining Momentum:

Summer.fi (https://summer.fi): Advanced DeFi management platform offering sophisticated portfolio optimization

Instadapp (https://instadapp.io/): DeFi infrastructure layer enabling complex multi-protocol strategies

SECRET #21: Asset Management Solutions - The New Hedge Fund Revolution

Enzyme Finance - The Institutional DeFi Revolution

Website: https://enzyme.finance/

Focus: On-chain asset management infrastructure

Features: Customizable investment strategies, risk management

US Access: Available to Americans with regulatory compliance

International Advantage: Global managers can create funds with fewer restrictions

dHedge Protocol - Decentralized Hedge Fund Infrastructure

Website: https://dhedge.org/

Focus: Performance tracking, manager incentives

US Limitation: Restricted access for US retail investors

International Freedom: Full access to sophisticated investment strategies

Yearn Finance - The Yield Farming Optimizer

Website: https://yearn.fi/

Focus: Automated yield optimization strategies

Features: Automated strategy execution, risk assessment

Global Reality: International users can access all vaults, Americans face some restrictions

The Geographic Arbitrage Secret: International users can participate in yield farming strategies that generate 10-50% APY through sophisticated multi-protocol compositions that Americans are often restricted from accessing.

SECRET #22: Decentralized Exchanges - The Freedom Network

Uniswap - The Regulatory Victory

Website: https://uniswap.org/

Status: Regulatory clarity achieved in 2025 when SEC closed its investigation without enforcement action

Features: Concentrated liquidity, multi-chain deployment

US Access: Fully available to Americans following regulatory clarity

International Advantage: Always had unrestricted global access

The Secret: Uniswap's victory sets the precedent that truly decentralized exchanges cannot be shut down by regulators, paving the way for the entire DEX ecosystem.

PancakeSwap - The BNB Chain Ecosystem

Website: https://pancakeswap.finance/

Focus: BNB Chain ecosystem optimization

Features: Yield farming, lottery, NFT marketplace

Geographic Reality: Fully accessible globally, including to Americans

1inch Network - The Optimization Engine

Website: https://1inch.io/

Focus: DEX aggregation and optimization

Features: Pathfinder algorithm, gas optimization

US Status: Fully accessible following 2025 regulatory improvements

Exploring DeFi Innovators: Companies and Tokens Shaping the Future

Introduction: This Ain't Just Tech - This Is the Shift

We are living in one of the greatest transitions of our lifetime. As the financial world shakes off its old skin, a new economy is emerging open, borderless, and driven by code instead of control.

This section isn't just a list. It's a spotlight on the rebels, the builders, and the visionaries rewriting the rules of money. These aren't just companies and protocols they're weapons of financial liberation.

Some are already walking through Wall Street's front door. Others are still building in the digital trenches. But all of them? They're shaping the world that Bit Main Street was born to thrive in.

And trust me as DeFi grows and the stablecoin space gets more regulated and more invasive, we're going to see something unexpected:

Projects that were once pure DeFi creeping into TradFi

The underground becoming the new standard

The margins moving to the center

This is your call to stay sharp. Stay curious. Keep your ears to the street and your eyes on the code.

The Bold Ones: Publicly Visible, Already Making Waves

These companies made it into the system, but don't get it twisted, they're here to shake it up. And the difference between now and 2018 is at least now we know how to vet companies we believe in.

Coinbase (COIN)

The front door to crypto for millions. On NASDAQ but still flying the flag for decentralized access.

Galaxy Digital (GLXY)
A digital bank built for this new world trading, mining, investing... all on-chain.

Riot Blockchain (RIOT)
Big-time Bitcoin mining power in the U.S., keeping the heartbeat of the network alive.

Animoca Brands (formerly ASX: AB1)
Metaverse and NFT investor with heavy hitters like The Sandbox. Quiet now, but planning a loud return with a U.S. IPO.

Circle
Issuer of USDC. Deeply plugged into U.S. crypto policy. If they go public, that's a move worth watching.

The True Builders: Protocols That Don't Ask Permission

Now let's talk real DeFi where people run the show, not suits. These aren't stocks. These are ecosystems. They don't need a boardroom to change the game:

Uniswap (UNI)

The OG DEX. Billions in liquidity. No middleman. Pure freedom.

Aave (AAVE)

Borrow and lend without a bank. No applications. No gatekeepers. Just smart contracts.

Compound (COMP)

Your money earns while you sleep because DeFi don't take lunch breaks.

SushiSwap (SUSHI)

Built by the community, for the community.

Curve Finance (CRV)

If you're swapping stablecoins and want low slippage, this is the smooth operator.

1inch (1INCH)

Finds the best deals across all DEXs. It's like having a DeFi deal sniper on your team.

Balancer (BAL)

Automated portfolio management that bends to your strategy, not the other way around.

PancakeSwap (CAKE)

Binance Smart Chain's low-fee playground. Cute branding, serious power.

How to Use This List: Don't Watch the Wave Surf It

This list isn't here to tell you what to buy. It's here to help you see the patterns. It's a compass for creators, entrepreneurs, students, and future DeFi Jedi.

Some of these names are going public. Some already are. Others will stay decentralized forever. But all of them carry a lesson on how new systems beat old ones not by knocking, but by building a new door.

Use this to inspire your next move. Your next lesson. Your next venture.

Because the future isn't coming.

You're building it.

The International Freedom Advantage

Countries Leading DeFi Adoption:

Switzerland: Clear regulatory framework, crypto-friendly banks

Singapore: Sandbox approach allowing DeFi experimentation

UAE: Progressive crypto laws attracting global talent

Portugal: Favorable tax treatment for crypto activities

Estonia: Digital residency enabling global DeFi participation

What International Users Enjoy:

Unrestricted Platform Access: No geographic blocking or VPN requirements

Full Feature Sets: Access to all protocol features without compliance limitations

Tax Optimization: Many jurisdictions offer favorable crypto tax treatment

Regulatory Clarity: Clear rules rather than enforcement uncertainty

Banking Integration: Crypto-friendly banks enabling easy fiat on/off ramps

The American Renaissance - Things Are Looking Up

Recent Positive Changes for US Users:

DeFi Reporting Relief: Nullification of burdensome reporting requirements for true DeFi protocols

SEC Innovation Exemptions: New framework recognizing truly decentralized protocols

GENIUS Act: Comprehensive stable-coin regulation providing legal clarity

Trump Administration Support: Presidential endorsement of crypto innovation

The New American Reality: While Americans have historically faced more restrictions than international users, the tide is turning. The 2025 regulatory changes represent the biggest shift toward crypto freedom in US history. Americans can now:

- Use truly decentralized protocols without reporting burdens
- Participate in DeFi lending and yield farming with legal clarity
- Trade on decentralized exchanges without regulatory uncertainty

- Hold stable-coins with proper regulatory backing

The Geographic Secret: Smart Americans are establishing international structures to access the full spectrum of DeFi opportunities while remaining compliant with US law. International users continue to enjoy unrestricted access to the most innovative financial protocols ever created.

Bottom Line: While the United States is finally embracing DeFi innovation, users outside America have always had more financial freedom and continue to enjoy broader access to cutting-edge protocols. However, for the first time since DeFi's inception, Americans can participate in this financial revolution without fear of regulatory persecution.

The path to true financial sovereignty requires understanding both the opportunities and limitations of your geographic location and knowing how to navigate them legally and effectively.

Chapter 6

The Security Codes -
Protection Secrets They
Don't Want You to Know

*"Navigate Web3 like a pro tactical guidance to
grow, protect, and multiply your crypto assets."*

The $2.4 Trillion Fortress That Has Never Been Broken

The Ultimate Security Benchmark

Here's a mind-blowing fact that puts everything in perspective: The Bitcoin blockchain has secured over $2.4 trillion (*as of August 8th 2025*) in value for more than 16 years without a single successful hack of its core protocol. Not once. While banks get robbed, credit card systems get breached, and even government databases get compromised, Bitcoin's blockchain has remained impenetrable.

This isn't luck it's mathematical certainty backed by the most powerful distributed computing network ever created.

The Power of Proof-of-Work Security: Bitcoin's security comes from approximately 500 exahashes per second (EH/s) of computational power more computing power than the world's top 500 supercomputers combined, multiplied by millions. To attack Bitcoin, you'd need to control more computing power than entire nations possess, making it practically impossible and economically irrational.

But here's where it gets interesting for DeFi users: this fortress-level security is now available for your financial transactions.

SECRET #23: The Tale of Two Blockchains - BTC vs ETH and the Power of Their Union

Bitcoin (BTC) - The Impenetrable Vault

Security Model: Proof-of-Work with 16+ years of battle-testing

Primary Function: Store of value and final settlement layer

Strengths: Unmatched security, simplicity, decentralization

Limitations: Limited smart contract capabilities, slower transaction speeds

Ethereum (ETH) - The Programmable Computer

Security Model: Proof-of-Stake with advanced smart contract capabilities

Primary Function: Decentralized computing platform and DeFi ecosystem

Strengths: Programmability, vast ecosystem, innovation speed

Trade-offs: More complex attack vectors, higher gas fees

The Revolutionary Combination: Modern DeFi protocols are now leveraging both blockchains through cross-chain bridges and Layer 2 solutions, creating systems that combine Bitcoin's security with Ethereum's programmability. This gives you:

- Bitcoin-level security for final settlement
- Ethereum-level flexibility for complex financial operations
- Cross-chain liquidity maximizing capital efficiency
- Risk diversification across multiple blockchain ecosystems

SECRET #24: Smart Contract Security - The Real Threat Landscape

The March 2025 Wake-Up Call

Smart contract breaches, in which bad actors exploit bugs in a service's code, and front-end attacks, where a user interface is altered to redirect funds into a hacker's wallet, remain primary concerns in DeFi. The SIR.trading DeFi protocol experienced a logic flaw attack in March 2025 that resulted in the theft of around $355,000 a stark reminder that even audited protocols can have vulnerabilities.

But here's the secret: these attacks target implementation flaws, not the underlying blockchain security. The Bitcoin and Ethereum blockchains themselves remained completely secure during these incidents.

Common Vulnerabilities Exposed:

1. Reentrancy Attacks - The $60 Million Lesson

Token contracts require safeguards against vulnerabilities like re-entrancy attacks, integer overflows, and unchecked external calls. The infamous DAO hack of 2016 taught the entire industry about reentrancy risks, leading to strategies such as the nonReentrant modifier and the Check-Effects-Interactions pattern.

The Secret Defense: Modern protocols implement state changes before external calls, preventing attackers from repeatedly calling functions before previous executions complete.

2. Oracle Manipulation - The Price Feed Deception

Price feed manipulation can lead to incorrect liquidations or arbitrage opportunities for attackers. Unlike Bitcoin's simple UTXO model, DeFi protocols rely on external price data, creating attack vectors.

The Secret Solution: Multi-oracle systems and time-weighted average prices (TWAP) make manipulation exponentially more expensive and difficult.

3. Front-End Compromises - The Interface Illusion

Malicious code injection into protocol interfaces can redirect user funds to attacker wallets. This is the most insidious attack because the blockchain protocol remains secure while users interact with compromised interfaces.

The Secret Protection: Always verify contract addresses through multiple sources and use hardware wallets that display transaction details.

SECRET #25: The Bitcoin-Ethereum Security Synthesis

Why the Combination Creates Ultimate Protection

Smart DeFi users are now leveraging protocols that combine both blockchain's strengths:

Bitcoin Integration Benefits:

- Wrapped Bitcoin (WBTC) brings Bitcoin's security to Ethereum DeFi
- Lightning Network integration enables instant, low-cost Bitcoin transactions
- Bitcoin-backed loans provide liquidity without selling BTC
- Cross-chain bridges allow Bitcoin holders to earn DeFi yields

Ethereum Enhancement Features:

- Smart contract automation eliminates counterparty risk
- Programmable money creates complex financial instruments
- Composability allows protocols to build on each other
- Transparent execution makes all operations verifiable

The Combined Power: Protocols like THORChain, RenProtocol, and newer Bitcoin DeFi solutions create systems where:

- Your Bitcoin remains secured by the world's most powerful network
- Your transactions execute with Ethereum's programmable flexibility
- Your funds benefit from both ecosystems' liquidity
- Your risks are distributed across multiple security models

SECRET #26: Mitigation Strategies That Actually Work

The Professional-Grade Security Framework

Always verify contract addresses through official channels: Use multiple sources including official websites, block explorers, and community verification. Attackers often create fake interfaces with slight URL variations.

Use hardware wallets for significant amounts: Ledger and Trezor devices provide air-gapped security that's immune to software-based attacks. Your private keys never touch internet-connected devices.

Monitor transaction details before signing: Hardware wallets display exact contract addresses and function calls. Never sign transactions you don't fully understand.

Diversify across multiple protocols: Don't put all funds in a single protocol, regardless of its reputation. Even the most secure protocols can have undiscovered vulnerabilities.

Stay informed about protocol updates and security incidents: Follow official channels, security researchers, and audit firms for real-time threat intelligence.

SECRET #27: Operational Security Guidelines - Military-Grade Protection

Wallet Security Architecture:

- Hardware wallets (Ledger, Trezor) for long-term storage and high-value transactions
- Hot wallets only for small amounts and frequent trading
- Multi-signature setups for institutional or high-value holdings
- Regular security audits of wallet access and permissions

Transaction Safety Protocols:

- Independent verification of recipient addresses through multiple channels
- Simulation tools (like Tenderly) before executing complex transactions
- Spending limits and time delays for large transactions
- Activity monitoring for unusual patterns or unauthorized access

Privacy and Operational Security:

- **Transaction traceability awareness:** All blockchain transactions are public
- **Privacy-focused tools:** Like Tornado Cash (where legally permissible)
- **Public address management:** Avoid linking multiple addresses to your identity
- **VPN usage:** For additional privacy layers when accessing DeFi protocols

The Bitcoin-Ethereum DeFi Security Model

The Ultimate Protection Strategy:

- Store long-term wealth in Bitcoin for maximum security
- Use Ethereum DeFi for active yield generation and trading
- Bridge between chains strategically to optimize security and returns
- Implement hardware wallet security for all significant transactions
- Diversify across protocols to minimize single points of failure

- Stay informed about emerging threats and security best practices

The Secret Truth: The combination of Bitcoin's battle-tested security with Ethereum's innovative DeFi ecosystem creates the most robust financial infrastructure ever built. While individual protocols may have vulnerabilities, the underlying blockchain systems provide security that surpasses traditional financial institutions.

By understanding and implementing these security codes, you're not just protecting your assets you're participating in the most secure financial system in human history.

Next, we'll explore how the 2025 regulatory landscape creates both opportunities and challenges for DeFi users navigating compliance requirements across different jurisdictions.

Chapter 7

The Legal Labyrinth - Regulatory Secrets and Compliance Codes

"Discover how to make Web3 work for you with clear, no-fluff guidance toward financial freedom."

Operation Choke Point 2.0: The Deliberate Destruction Campaign Exposed

The Most Unethical Attack on American Financial Freedom

Here's a story that will make your blood boil: For nearly four years, Gary Gensler and the SEC deliberately orchestrated what insiders call "Operation Choke Point 2.0" a coordinated government effort to destroy the American crypto industry through regulatory warfare, banking restrictions, and enforcement terrorism.

This wasn't regulatory oversight. This was economic warfare.

The Smoking Gun Evidence: When confronted by Rep. Warren Davidson (R-OH) about Operation Choke Point 2.0, Gary Gensler claimed, "I've never heard that term," smiling as he denied knowledge of the very program his agency was executing. This lie was exposed when law firm Cooper & Kirk, the same firm that successfully sued to stop the original Operation Choke Point, published a devastating white paper proving the coordinated attack.

The Systematic Destruction Strategy:

1. **Banking Deplatforming:** Regulators pressured banks to stop serving crypto companies, destroying their financial infrastructure

2. **Regulatory Limbo:** Deliberately avoiding clear regulations to keep the industry in legal uncertainty

3. **Enforcement Terrorism:** Launching dubious lawsuits designed to bankrupt companies through legal costs

4. **Media Manipulation:** Coordinating negative narratives to destroy public confidence

The Personal Vendetta Revealed: Gensler's true feelings became crystal clear when he announced the SEC's lawsuit against Coinbase: "We don't need more digital currency. We already have digital currency. It's called the U.S. dollar. It's called the euro. It's called the yen."

This wasn't about consumer protection it was about protecting the traditional financial system from disruption.

SECRET #28: The Choke Point Casualties - Billions in Damage

The Human Cost of Regulatory Warfare

Chris Lane, former CTO of Silvergate Bank, revealed the brutal reality: "FTX didn't kill us. Regulators did." Despite surviving a 70% deposit run after the FTX collapse, regulatory pressure destroyed the bank that served as a critical infrastructure for legitimate crypto businesses.

The Debanking Campaign: Over 30 tech founders were systematically debanked, many from firms backed by Andreessen Horowitz. Marc Andreessen himself was debanked, calling it "an attack on individual freedom." Tyler Winklevoss confirmed he was "debanked because I'm in crypto."

Coinbase CEO Brian Armstrong's Accusation: "This was one of the most unethical and un-American things that happened in the Biden administration." Armstrong revealed that Coinbase filed Freedom of Information Act requests to expose the government's coordinated attack.

The Global Destruction: Charles Hoskinson called it a "coordinated global campaign against crypto" that "crushed businesses, stifled economies, and slowed innovation worldwide."

SECRET #29: The Avoidance Strategy - Keeping Markets in Legal Limbo

The Deliberate Ambiguity Tactic

Here's the most insidious part of Gensler's strategy: He deliberately avoided creating clear regulations to keep the crypto market in perpetual legal uncertainty. This wasn't incompetence it was calculated destruction.

The Enforcement-Only Approach: Instead of providing regulatory clarity, the SEC launched weekly enforcement actions, making it impossible for legitimate businesses to know what was legal.

Companies like Coinbase begged for clear rules, only to be met with lawsuits.

The Howey Test Weaponization: Gensler misapplied the 1946 Howey Test to modern blockchain technology, leading to his public humiliation when a federal judge scolded him for misapplying the law in the Ripple case.

The Congressional Testimony Disaster: During his September 2024 appearance before Congress, Rep. Tom Emmer declared: "We could not have had a more historically destructive or lawless Chairman of the SEC."

SECRET #30: Strategic Implementation - How to Profit from the Regulatory Revolution

Beyond the Headlines: Actionable Investment Intelligence

While Chapter 3 covered what the 2025 regulatory changes mean, this secret reveals exactly how to profit from their implementation. *The GENIUS Act,*

CLARITY Act, and Anti-CBDC Act create specific wealth opportunities for those who understand the strategic implications.

The Corporate Stablecoin Gold Rush: Your Investment Roadmap

Corporate Stablecoin Launch Timeline (2025-2026):

Amazon Pay Coin (APC): Q4 2025 launch rumored, Treasury-backed for Prime transactions
Investment Strategy: Monitor AWS blockchain services, Ethereum Layer 2 partnerships

Walmart Digital Dollar (WDD): Supply chain settlements and employee payments
Play: Watch VeChain partnerships, supply chain blockchain investments

JPMorgan Public Coin (JPC): Consumer version of JPM Coin for retail banking
Angle: Track Ethereum enterprise adoption, Quorum blockchain development

PayPal USD 2.0: GENIUS Act compliant upgrade to existing PYUSD
Strategy: Position before institutional payment adoption accelerates

Implementation Timeline: Your Strategic Windows

Q3-Q4 2025: The Compliance Rush

Stablecoin Consolidation: Smaller issuers acquired by Circle, Paxos, and new corporate entrants

Protocol Upgrades: DeFi platforms implementing compliance features trigger price movements

Exchange Positioning: Platforms building CFTC-compliant infrastructure gain competitive advantages

Investment Strategy: Position in protocols before institutional capital floods in

CLARITY Act Investment Opportunities

Smart money is positioning for CLARITY Act benefits:

Token Reclassification Plays: *Projects moving from SEC to CFTC oversight*
Opportunity: Find protocols making this transition early

$75M Safe Harbor Sales: *New fundraising sweet spot for compliant projects*
Strategy: Participate in compliant token sales under the threshold

Utility Token Premium: *Clear utility classification creates valuation advantages*
Play: Research tokens likely to benefit from favorable definitions

Anti-CBDC Act: Hidden Investment Advantages

Private Stablecoin Monopoly: *No government competition increases demand*
Investment: Circle (USDC), Paxos (USDP) benefit from reduced competition

DeFi Permanent Advantage: *Protocols remain the only alternative to banking*
Strategy: DeFi protocols gain unassailable competitive moats

Privacy Premium Valuations: *Non-surveillance tools command higher prices*
Opportunity: Privacy-focused protocols become institutional grade

Tax Optimization Implementation

The April 2025 legislation creates actionable tax strategies:

DeFi Tax Advantages You Can Implement:

Yield Farming Clarity: Multi-protocol strategies now have clear tax treatment
Action: Implement complex yield optimization with predictable obligations

Cross-Chain Relief: Bridge operations avoid burdensome reporting
Strategy: Execute cross-chain arbitrage strategies legally

DAO Participation Benefits: Governance activities get favorable treatment
Play: Active governance participation becomes tax-advantaged

Staking Income Rules: Compliant protocols offer tax efficiency
Opportunity: Focus staking on GENIUS Act compliant platforms

SEC Framework Investment Opportunities

The "DeFi and the American Spirit" framework creates specific plays:

AMM Safe Harbor Protocols: Uniswap-style platforms get regulatory protection
Strategy: Focus on truly decentralized AMM protocols

Flash Loan Advantage: *Uncollateralized lending gets innovation protection*
Investment: Platforms offering flash loans gain regulatory moats

Governance Token Protection: *Decentralized governance avoids securities rules*
Play: Identify protocols with genuine community governance

2028 Bitcoin Halving Positioning

Regulatory clarity creates explosive 2028 opportunities:

Compliant Protocol Premium: Regulated platforms command 50-200% valuation premiums

Institutional Capital Tsunami: $2-5 trillion in traditional finance entering DeFi

Innovation Acceleration: Clear rules enable sophisticated products by 2028

Global Standard Setting: US protocols become international benchmarks

Your 5-Step Strategic Action Plan:

1. **Q3 2025:** Position in protocols benefiting from corporate stablecoin adoption

2. **Q4 2025:** Participate in CLARITY Act compliant token sales under $75M

3. **2026:** Implement cross-chain yield strategies with new tax advantages

4. **2027:** Scale positions preparing for institutional adoption wave

5. **2028:** Execute maximum gains during Bitcoin halving institutional FOMO

The regulatory revolution creates the biggest wealth transfer opportunity in crypto history. Those who understand implementation details will capture disproportionate gains while others remain confused by headlines.

SECRET #31: The Choke Point Investigation - Justice Finally Coming

David Sacks' Investigation Promise

White House Crypto and AI Czar David Sacks has committed to investigating Operation Choke Point 2.0, stating: "There are too many stories of people being hurt by Operation Choke Point 2.0. It needs to be looked at."

The Evidence Being Uncovered:

FOIA requests revealing government coordination: Coinbase and other companies are exposing internal communications

Banking regulator violations: Cooper & Kirk argues regulators violated Due Process Clause of Fifth Amendment

Unconstitutional targeting: The systematic debanking of legal businesses without due process

Industry-wide damage assessment: Quantifying the billions in losses from regulatory warfare

Congressional Action Demanded: The Cooper & Kirk white paper calls on Congress to:

- Require bank regulators to submit communications about crypto restrictions
- Explain the basis for conclusions about crypto's threat to financial stability
- Hold regulators accountable for illegal actions against legitimate businesses

SECRET #32: Best Practices for Compliance in the New Era

The Professional Survival Guide

1. Documentation - Your Legal Shield: Maintain detailed records of all DeFi activities, including:

- Transaction timestamps and amounts
- Protocol interactions and yield farming activities
- Cross-chain bridge operations
- Staking and governance participation

2. Professional Guidance - Expert Navigation: Consult with crypto-knowledgeable tax professionals who understand:

- The April 2025 reporting exemptions for DeFi protocols
- State-by-state compliance variations
- International structure opportunities
- Emerging regulatory interpretations

3. Regular Reviews - Staying Current: Stay updated on regulatory changes through:

- Official SEC and Treasury guidance

- Industry trade association updates
- Legal precedents from ongoing court cases
- International regulatory developments

4. Risk Assessment - Legal and Financial:
Evaluate legal risks alongside financial risks by:

- Assessing protocol decentralization levels
- Understanding jurisdiction-specific requirements
- Monitoring enforcement actions and precedents
- Maintaining compliance documentation

The New American Reality: From Choke Point to Freedom Point

The Transformation Complete

The contrast is staggering: In 2023, legitimate crypto businesses were being systematically destroyed through regulatory warfare. By 2025, the President of the United States launched his own cryptocurrency token and achieved a $15 billion market cap.

What This Means for DeFi Users:

- **Legal Clarity:** True DeFi protocols now have regulatory protection
- **Banking Access:** The systematic debanking campaign has ended
- **Innovation Freedom:** Developers can build without fear of arbitrary enforcement
- **International Competitiveness:** America is finally competing rather than self-destructing

The Gensler Legacy: Gary Gensler's "historically destructive" tenure will be remembered as the darkest period in American financial regulation—a cautionary tale of what happens when regulators prioritize control over innovation.

The Path Forward: Understanding this history isn't just about the past—it's about recognizing that regulatory environments can change rapidly, and prepared users can thrive regardless of political winds.

The secret to long-term success in DeFi is building compliance frameworks that work across jurisdictions and regulatory cycles, ensuring you can operate legally whether regulators are hostile or friendly.

Chapter 8

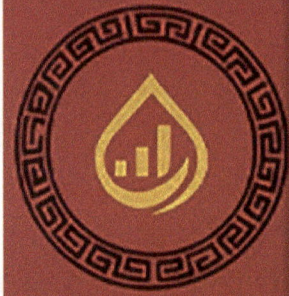

THE MASTER'S
PLAYBOOK

Advanced DeFi Strategies Unveiled

孫子 史法

The Master's Playbook - Advanced DeFi Strategies Unveiled

" The DeFi Jedi Crypto Academy: The Path to Financial Freedom"

The Path to Financial Freedom - Your Complete Education System

Ten Years of DeFi Evolution: From Hope to Reality to Solution

The Ethereum blockchain was launched in 2015, and since then, thousands of smart contracts have been developed. The decentralized application industry has grown from hope to reality to the solution, and now in 2025 ten years later I believe this new economy can bring us the financial freedom we all strive to achieve.

We've moved past theory. The code works. The systems scale. The adoption is real.

And now, the question isn't *"Will DeFi change the world?"* it's *"Will you be ready when it does?"*

Here's the hard truth:

Earning significant returns in DeFi **is not gambling**. It's a skillset one that must be learned, practiced, and mastered. That's why I created **The DeFi Jedi Crypto Academy,** a complete, battle-tested education system for turning intermediate users into confident, disciplined DeFi professionals.

The DeFi Jedi Crypto Academy

Your Complete Path to Financial Freedom

This isn't a crash course. It's a *playbook* forged from ten years of real-world blockchain experience, market analysis, and the lessons of every bull and bear cycle since Ethereum's genesis block.

PART 1: The Fundamentals

Everything you need to know to make money in DeFi built on the foundation we've laid in the previous chapters:

- Regulatory clarity and how to use it to your advantage
- The security protocols that keep you in the game when others get liquidated
- Understanding market dynamics so you never move blind

PART 2: Wallet Security & Environment Setup

No serious player starts without armor. We'll cover:

- Bitcoin-Ethereum hybrid security synthesis (from Chapter 4)

- Air-gapping, multi-sig, and cold storage setups
- Creating a safe working environment so your profits aren't just made — they're protected

PART 3: Market Intelligence & Bull Market Strategies

Here's where we start *winning the game before it starts*:

- My proprietary system for reading **CoinMarketCap** is like a pro
- Identifying early momentum before the mainstream piles in
- Strategies for thriving in the 2025 *Regulatory Renaissance* bull run

PART 4: Alpha Token Identification

Spotting the next 100x or 1000x token is not luck — it's research discipline:

- How to filter noise and find real projects with asymmetric upside
- Risk management frameworks that let you swing big without going broke

- Multiple real-world examples from past cycles

PART 5: The DeFi Jedi Mastermind Group *(Invitation Only)*

This is the inner circle. The war room. The place where strategy becomes reality:

- Access via the **Decentralized Sovereign Network**
- Private newsletter and exclusive research drops
- Crypto paywall-protected alpha strategies
- Live conference calls and collaborative builds
- Training on how to develop **your own mastermind network** to multiply opportunities

Your Next Move

I can't make the market move for you.

But I can give you the training, the tools, and the network so you can move with precision when it does.

All I ask is that you bring:

- **Faith** - in the technology, in the process, and in your ability to learn
- **Patience** - because mastery takes time
- **Discipline** - because even the best strategies fail without execution
- **A willingness to learn** - because the game changes fast

If you have these, the DeFi Jedi path is open to you.

Thank you for trusting me to guide you through this new frontier.

The next chapters will take everything we've covered — from the warnings to the wins — and forge them into your personal **Master Playbook for DeFi Freedom**.

SECRET #33: Yield Optimization Techniques - The Money-Making Machine

Automated Strategy Platforms: The Professional's Toolkit

Now that you understand the regulatory landscape and security fundamentals, let's explore how to generate serious returns through yield optimization:

Yearn Finance Vaults - The Hands-Off Fortune Builder

Website: https://yearn.fi/

Strategy: Automated yield farming with professional-grade optimization

2025 Advantage: Benefiting from new regulatory clarity and institutional adoption

Returns: 8-25% APY on stablecoins, 15-50% on volatile assets during bull markets

Secret: Yearn's strategies automatically compound returns and optimize gas costs across multiple protocols

Harvest Finance - The Yield Aggregation Engine

Focus: Optimized yield aggregation across farming opportunities

Strategy: Automatically harvests and compounds rewards from multiple farms

Edge: Professional-grade strategies previously available only to institutions

2025 Update: Enhanced with cross-chain opportunities and regulatory-compliant protocols

Convex Finance - The Curve Protocol Maximizer

Specialization: Curve protocol optimization and enhanced CRV rewards

Mechanism: Locks CRV tokens to boost yields and earn trading fees

Returns: 20-100% APY during optimal market conditions

Professional Secret: Convex allows smaller investors to access the same yield boosts as whales

Manual Strategy Development - The Alpha Advantage

For intermediate users ready to maximize returns through active management:

Cross-Protocol Yield Comparison: Use platforms like DeFi Pulse and DeBank to compare yields across Aave, Compound, and newer protocols. The secret is identifying temporary yield spikes before they normalize.

Impermanent Loss Calculation and Mitigation:

Use tools like impermanent-loss.com to calculate risk/reward ratios

Implement delta-neutral strategies using options and perpetual swaps

Focus on correlated pairs (ETH/stETH) to minimize impermanent loss

Gas Cost Optimization:

Use Layer 2 solutions (Arbitrum, Optimism, Polygon) for small transactions

Batch transactions during low-gas periods (weekends, early mornings UTC)

Utilize gas trackers and set appropriate limits to avoid failed transactions

SECRET #34: Portfolio Diversification - The Risk Management Matrix

Advanced Risk Management Framework

Protocol Diversification Strategy:

Established Protocols (60-70%): Aave, Compound, MakerDAO, Uniswap— battle-tested with regulatory clarity

Emerging Platforms (20-30%): Summer.fi, Instadapp, newer Layer 2 protocols with higher yields

Experimental Positions (5-10%): New protocols with extraordinary yields but higher risks

Balance Established vs. Emerging Platforms:

Blue-chip DeFi: Lower yields (5-15%) but maximum security and liquidity

Mid-tier protocols: Moderate yields (15-35%) with proven track records

New protocols: High yields (35-200%) but require extensive due diligence

Correlation Analysis: Avoid concentrated exposure to correlated yield sources. For example, don't put your entire portfolio in Curve-based strategies, as they'll all suffer during CRV price crashes.

Geographic and Regulatory Diversification

Multi-Chain Deployment Strategies:

Ethereum Mainnet: Primary security and liquidity hub

Layer 2 Solutions: Arbitrum and Optimism for cost-effective strategies

Alternative Chains: Polygon, Avalanche, BSC for higher yields and diversification

Bitcoin Integration: Wrapped Bitcoin strategies and Lightning Network opportunities

Regulatory Risk Mitigation:

Jurisdiction Diversification: Protocols governed by different regulatory frameworks

Compliance Monitoring: Track which protocols meet 2025 regulatory standards

Exit Strategies: Maintain ability to quickly move funds across jurisdictions

Currency Exposure Management:

USD Exposure: Stablecoin farming for predictable returns

ETH/BTC Exposure: Native token strategies for upside participation

Alt-coin Exposure: Carefully selected high-growth potential tokens

SECRET #35: Cross-Chain Operations - The Advanced Profit Engine

Bridge Security and Multi-Chain Mastery

Bridge Protocol Evaluation Framework:

Security Audits: Only use bridges with multiple recent audits

TVL Analysis: Higher Total Value Locked indicates market confidence

Insurance Coverage: Protocols with insurance (Nexus Mutual, InsurAce) preferred

Track Record: Avoid bridges with history of exploits or technical issues

Professional Bridge Selection:

Ethereum ↔ Layer 2: Native bridges (Arbitrum, Optimism) offer maximum security

Ethereum ↔ Other Chains: Multichain, Synapse, or Hop Protocol for established routes

Emergency Bridges: Always have backup bridging options in case primary bridges fail

Multi-Chain Arbitrage Strategies:

Cross-Chain Yield Arbitrage:

Monitor identical protocols on different chains for yield discrepancies

Example: Aave on Ethereum vs. Aave on Polygon often shows 2-5% yield differences

Factor in bridge costs and slippage when calculating profitability

Liquidity Provision Arbitrage:

Provide liquidity on multiple networks for the same token pairs

Take advantage of volume surges on specific chains

Rebalance liquidity based on fee generation and incentive programs

Gas Optimization Across Chains:

Ethereum: Use during low-gas periods, batch transactions

Polygon: Micro-strategies viable due to low gas costs

Arbitrum/Optimism: Sweet spot for medium-sized positions

BSC/Avalanche: High-yield opportunities with moderate gas costs

The Decentralized Sovereign Network – Your Gateway to Alpha

Where Education Meets Execution

The strategies you've seen so far are just the tip of the spear. The real magic happens when you combine knowledge, timing, and community. That's exactly what the Decentralized Sovereign Network was built for a members-only command center where serious DeFi players sharpen their edge, find alpha before the crowd, and act with confidence.

This isn't a Telegram group full of hype posts. It's a living intelligence network a place where every member contributes, and every call, document, and connection is designed to increase your financial sovereignty.

1. Weekly Alpha Calls – Strategy in Real Time

Every week, we go live to break down the market before the rest of the world reacts.

You'll get:

- **Emerging Protocol Analysis & Risk Assessment** - Spot the gems early, skip the landmines.
- **Real-Time Market Opportunities & Threat Identification** - Enter early, exit smart.
- **Cross-Chain Arbitrage Opportunities** - Move capital between blockchains in minutes for outsized gains.
- **Regulatory Updates with Tactical Plays** - Turn rule changes into advantages instead of roadblocks.

2. Private Newsletter Intelligence – Professional-Grade Research

Delivered straight to your secure inbox, this isn't fluff — it's actionable intel you can trade on:

- **Protocol Security Assessments Before Public Release -** Never get rugged because you missed a code audit.
- **Yield Farming Opportunities in Pre-Launch Phases -** Position before APRs collapse.
- **Regulatory Arbitrage Strategies for International Users -** Play the rules to your advantage, no matter your jurisdiction.

Deep Technical Analysis of Emerging DeFi Innovations Understand the "why" behind the hype.

3. Mastermind Network Development – Power in Numbers

No serious alpha hunter works alone. Inside the Decentralized Sovereign Network, you'll:

- Connect with High-Level DeFi Professionals – Cut through the noise and network with real builders and investors.

- Share Due Diligence & Risk Assessments — Two minds are good. Ten are unstoppable.
- Collaborate on Large-Scale Strategies — Execute plays that require liquidity pools bigger than any one member could move alone.
- Gain Exclusive Deal Flow & Early Access Opportunities — Be in the room before the door even opens to the public.

Why This Matters

In the old financial world, access to real intelligence was reserved for hedge funds, institutions, and insiders. The Decentralized Sovereign Network flips that script. It puts you the individual at the center of the action with the same quality of research, coordination, and execution the pros use.

When others are guessing, you'll be planning.

When others are chasing, you'll be positioned.

The 2028 DeFi Advantage: Regulatory Clarity Meets Innovation

Why Now Is the Perfect Time

The combination of regulatory clarity, institutional adoption, and technological maturation creates unprecedented opportunities for DeFi users:

Institutional Capital Inflow: Traditional finance is finally entering DeFi, providing deeper liquidity and more stable yields.

Regulatory Protection: True DeFi protocols now have legal clarity, reducing platform risk significantly.

Technology Maturation: Cross-chain infrastructure, Layer 2 scaling, and security improvements make sophisticated strategies accessible to intermediate users.

Market Inefficiencies: The regulatory destruction of 2022-2024 created market inefficiencies that educated users can exploit for extraordinary returns.

The 2028 Bitcoin Halving Catalyst: The Perfect Storm

Why 2028 Will Be the Greatest Crypto Boom in History

Looking ahead to 2028, we're positioning for what will likely be the most explosive crypto market cycle ever witnessed. Here's why the stars are aligning:

The Bitcoin Halving Effect: The 2028 Bitcoin halving will cut new supply in half while demand explodes. With the Gensler regime's regulatory destruction now behind us, and clear legal frameworks in place, institutional adoption will accelerate exponentially.

The Scarcity-Demand Explosion:

- **Pension Fund Participation:** Rumors of pension funds being allowed to participate in Bitcoin will create unprecedented institutional demand in a scarcity market
- **Difficulty Rate Increase:** As mining difficulty increases post-halving, the cost of producing new Bitcoin will force price appreciation
- **Industry Diversification:** Institutional capital will be forced to diversify beyond Bitcoin into DeFi

protocols, creating massive liquidity flows

The Innovation Explosion (2025-2028):

- **Thousands of New Protocols:** With regulatory clarity established, expect thousands of innovative DeFi protocols to launch in the next three years
- **Cross-Chain Maturation:** True interoperability will unlock liquidity across all major blockchains
- **Traditional Finance Integration:** Banks, hedge funds, and institutional investors will launch their own DeFi products
- **Yield Optimization Revolution:** Sophisticated yield strategies will become accessible to retail investors

Why the DeFi Jedi Mastermind Group Will Be Powerful

The members stepping into the Decentralized Sovereign Network today aren't here to chase trends they're here to shape them. By the time the mainstream wakes up to these shifts in 2028, our community will already have:

- **Three Years of Elite-Level DeFi Training & Execution** - Not just theory, but proven battle experience in live markets.
- **First-Mover Access to Emerging Protocols** - Positioning before the hype, where the real multiples live.
- **Deep Stakes in Battle-Tested Platforms** - Assets that survived the storms and grew stronger under pressure.
- **Network Effects with Other Heavy Hitters** - The kind of collaboration that multiplies profits beyond what any single player could achieve.
- **Fluent Command of Regulatory Frameworks** - Turning compliance from a barrier into a strategic weapon for wealth creation.

The 2028 Prediction

By the time the next Bitcoin halving strikes, DeFi will have shed its "experimental" label and become the invisible backbone of global finance. Those who have mastered these protocols *now* will be in prime position to ride the largest wealth transfer in modern history with the knowledge, positions, and network to capture the full wave.

The Bottom Line

The next era of advanced DeFi will merge:

- **The Security of Traditional Finance** - Capital protections that satisfy even the most cautious investor.
- **The Innovation of Decentralized Protocols** - Open, programmable, unstoppable financial systems.
- **The Muscle of Institutional Adoption** - Billions in capital pouring into ecosystems we've already mastered.
- **The Scarcity of Bitcoin** - A hard-cap asset driving value into every decentralized channel.

Victory won't belong to the gamblers. It will belong to the educated, disciplined, and connect those with access to professional-grade intelligence and the courage to act before the crowd.

If you're ready to transform your DeFi knowledge into a system that produces consistent profits... if you're ready to plant yourself at the epicenter of the 2028 boom... the Decentralized Sovereign Network is your gateway.

Chapter 9

The Sovereign Network - Building Your Web 3.0 Empire

"And also that nation, whom they shall serve, will I judge: and afterward shall they come out with great substance."

– Genesis 15:14

It's the summer of 2029.

The air feels different. The news feeds are filled with panic as centralized banks enforce new restrictions CBDC limits on purchases, rolling "emergency freezes" on accounts, and the slow, choking collapse of the old financial guard.

But you're calm. You're sitting on the balcony of your coastal home paid for in full, sipping coffee grown on a farm owned by one of your network partners. Your phone buzzes. It's a private DeFi alert from the Decentralized Sovereign Network another pre-launch protocol your team identified three weeks ago has just gone public… and your position is already up 420%.

You scroll through your portfolio. The assets you acquired before the 2025 boom the ones you learned to stake, farm, and protect in the early days now form the backbone of your wealth. Every token, every protocol, every position tells a story of foresight.

Your inbox is full not with bills or bank threats but with partnership requests from new Web 3.0 ventures, invitations to private mastermind summits, and updates from decentralized marketplaces you helped seed. Your name is whispered in circles that control the flow of entire blockchain economies.

You're not a spectator in this new financial world.

You helped *build* it.

And it all traces back to a moment *this* moment when you decided to step into sovereignty, learn the architecture, master the tools, and join a network that saw the future coming before anyone else.

Now, as the old-world burns and the fiat dollar is overtaken by BRICS, your empire thrives.

In this chapter, we'll break down the **Sovereign Network Blueprint** the exact framework for building, scaling, and defending your own Web 3.0 empire. From decentralized infrastructure to income streams that can't be frozen, you'll see how to take the principles we've explored and turn them into a living, breathing economic machine that belongs to you and you alone.

Because history doesn't remember the bystanders.

It remembers the builders.

The Great Offer: A New Business Opportunity Awaits

SECRET #36: From Dark Web to Light Web - The Ultimate Transformation

Understanding the Three Levels of Internet Freedom

Before we explore how to earn passive income through decentralized infrastructure, we need to understand the three levels of the internet:

1. **The Clearnet or surface web** is where you find Google, Facebook, Twitter, and most e-commerce.
2. **The Deep Web** is the bulk of the internet where you'll find university databases, legal documents, financial records, scientific data, and subscription databases.
3. **The Dark Web** is where you'll find political activism and, unfortunately, illegal activity. It's called the Dark Web because search engines cannot find these sites, they're built using IPv6 technology and can only be viewed using the Tor Browser.

But here's the revolutionary secret: Technology is not evil; what you do with the technology makes it good or evil.

A few years ago, I was introduced to the idea of how to turn the Dark Web into the Light Web and I was shown how to make passive income using this technology. In recent years, developers have started leveraging the Bitcoin network using Lightning Network and blockchain technology to build alternative platforms and services to those on the Clear Net.

The Light Web Revolution: We're building censorship-resistant, privacy-preserving infrastructure that serves humanity rather than exploiting it.

SECRET #37: The Legend of Zelda Principle - Knowledge Is Power

The Gaming Metaphor That Changes Everything

Freedom through the Decentralized Sovereign Network. If you've made it this far in this book, then you've already begun unlocking financial freedom and now it's time to unlock creative sovereignty.

As a child, I was captivated by adventure video games, especially *The Legend of Zelda*. I played as a young warrior on a quest to save the princess, exploring a vast world and collecting artifacts that gave me more and more power as I advanced. Every secret I uncovered gave me the tools I needed to overcome the next challenge. The deeper I ventured, the more unstoppable I became because knowledge was power.

In real life, the same principle applies. But here, the enemies are censorship, centralized control, and data exploitation. And your sword? It's understanding. Your shield? Sovereignty.

You now have that understanding. You've unlocked layers of decentralized infrastructure, peer-to-peer finance, and sovereign identity. But the final secret lies just behind the curtain, the Decentralized Sovereign Network isn't just a concept... it's the back end. It powers the infrastructure, it hosts your apps, and it now drives AI development in a privacy-respecting way.

So what's next? We bring that same sovereign power to creativity, authorship, and digital proof of ownership. Enter the next chapter of your journey.

SECRET #37.5: Help Wanted Web 3.0 Visionaries Needed

Ready to protect your genius the same way you protect your bitcoin?

The Problem:

As the world grows more aware of Bitcoin and the power of decentralized finance, the digital divide remains painfully clear. How do we empower the corner store on the south side, or the artist in a remote town, to fully tap into the blockchain revolution? How do we help low-income users who rely solely on mobile devices, in areas where blockchain still sounds like science fiction?

The Solution:

Employment through innovation. The bridge between mom-and-pop shops and the decentralized world is just one DApp away. We now have the ability to send files and execute contracts for pennies using Lightning Network tools like LNbits and BTCPay Server. With low-fee, fast blockchain functionality, we're unlocking global access to smart contracts, micropayments, and sovereign business models.

Picture this future job listing:

Advert of the Future: Now Hiring - Freedom Builders

"A brand new business opportunity awaits. Are you an entrepreneur? Do you have an eye for innovation and freedom? Then you're in the right place. As a Web 3.0 Full Stack Developer, I've spent years designing what I call a Sovereign Network a decentralized system built to restore ownership, privacy, and power to creators and builders around the world. Bit Main Street Sovereign Network isn't just a platform it's a movement. A space for kindred minds to gather, trade honestly, speak freely, and build lasting wealth on their own terms. It's where Web 3.0 business comes to life, running on tools you can host yourself. All it takes is a Raspberry Pi and the right guidance."

The infrastructure is here. The opportunity is real. And you already have what it takes."

If you've ever dreamed of reclaiming your digital rights, building a system of your own, and helping others escape the old gatekeepers this is your call to action. Let's go from consumer to creator, from client to controller.

SECRET #38: Immutable Copyright Registry via AI + Blockchain

IDEA - Proof of Creation in a Sovereign Age

In a world where content flies across the internet at light speed, creators need protection that's just as fast and permanent. The idea of copyright is ancient, but the enforcement has always been controlled by centralized powers. What if you could stamp your authorship onto the blockchain, powered by AI, without needing a middleman?

The Immutable Copyright Registry blends artificial intelligence, decentralized storage, and blockchain technology to create a new way for creators to claim what's theirs. And with optional NFT Artist Proofs, creators can finally lock their legacy into an unchangeable record.

The Opportunity: Immutable Copyright Registry via AI + Blockchain

The Idea

Imagine a platform where any creator — writer, artist, coder, or musician — can lock in proof of authorship instantly and permanently. No lawyers, no waiting, no central authority.

Here's the core concept:

- **Creator Platform:** Register writing, art, music, or code with blockchain protection.
- **AI Metadata:** Automatically generate title, tags, genre, and summary for precise classification.
- **Blockchain Proof:** Store a verifiable SHA256 hash on Arweave, IPFS, or Bitcoin via OpenTimestamps (OTS).
- **Public Record:** Make ownership provable through public blockchain entries.
- **NFT Option:** Optionally mint a Certificate of Authenticity or NFT for extra protection and value.

Key Features

- **AI Metadata Extractor:** Pulls essential details (title, author, genre, summary) directly from content.
- **File Hashing:** Uses SHA256 or IPFS CID for an immutable digital fingerprint.
- **Immutable Ledger:** Records the hash and timestamp on Bitcoin,

Arweave, or a hybrid blockchain setup.

- **QR + Certificate:** Issues a PDF certificate with a scannable QR code linking to the proof.
- **Verification Portal:** A public dashboard anyone can use to verify authorship instantly.
- **NFT Proof (Optional):** Mint works as NFTs for marketplace integration and collector value.

Monetization Strategy

1. **Freemium Model:** Offer 1–2 free registrations, then upsell premium features.
2. **Subscription Plans:** $10/month or a pay-per-upload credit system.
3. **Add-On Services:** Offer DMCA takedown kits, legal referrals, and smart contract templates.
4. **Enterprise Licensing:** Sell to publishers, universities, indie studios, and record labels.

Ideal Tech Stack

- **Frontend:** React.js or Vue.js for a fast, modern user interface.
- **Backend:** Node.js or ASP.NET Core for scalability.
- **Hashing:** SHA256, IPFS CID, or BLAKE3 for verifiable file fingerprints.
- **Blockchain Layer:** OpenTimestamps (BTC), Arweave, or Ethereum for recording proof.
- **Storage:** IPFS or Filebase for decentralized file hosting.
- **AI Integration:** GPT models or local LLMs (Mistral, Claude) for metadata generation.

Bonus: If You Already Have These, You're Halfway There

- IPFS
- BTCPay Server
- Filebase
- Ghost CMS + self-hosting

This system integrates perfectly as an add-on service for Bit Main Street or Satoshi For Storage, creating a new income layer built on sovereignty.

Killer Promo Angle

"Prove you created it. Time-stamp your creativity. Build your copyright shield in 60 seconds or less."

This is how you protect your genius and monetize it in one move.

Future AI Builder Prompts

User Flow Expansion
"Design a one-page onboarding that guides non-technical creators from upload to blockchain proof in under two minutes."

AI Enhancement
"Build a local LLM metadata extractor that works offline and integrates seamlessly with IPFS uploads."

Monetization Experiments
"Create an in-app marketplace for NFT proofs that allows direct-to-collector sales with Lightning Network payments."

Legal Integration
"Develop a DMCA auto-generation tool that takes blockchain proof and formats it into ready-to-send takedown requests."

Verification Expansion

"Build a public search engine that indexes all registered works for proof-of-existence queries."

Mobile-First Optimization
"Develop a mobile-friendly upload and verification flow for creators who rely solely on smartphones."

Using AI as a Tool to Build Your Web 3.0 Empire

As the rivalry between Sam Altman's OpenAI and Elon Musk's Colossus supercomputer intensifies, headlines are flooded with warnings: *AI is coming for your job.* With autonomous robots preparing to saturate the global workforce, the narrative feels urgent and real.

Already, NVIDIA chips are powering Tesla's in-house CPUs, fueling advancements that were once science fiction. We are witnessing the next great leap in human evolution not from horse and buggy to automobile, but from the automobile to an alternate reality once imagined by quantum physicists.

This isn't just a technological shift; it's a full-on paradigm change. And in this new era, those who learn to *work with AI*, not against it, will build the digital empires of tomorrow.

If you're anything like me, you've probably asked yourself: *Where do I fit in if my skills are becoming obsolete?* Are we all supposed to accept Universal Basic Income while we polish robots or manage the boring, low-risk tasks that machines haven't yet automated? Is that the future, humans reduced to system maintenance while the algorithms run the show?

Before this conversation crashes into the conspiracy swamp, let's steer it back toward the light. Because here's the truth: we're standing at the edge of a renaissance. A digital rebirth. One we can either harness or get permanently left behind by.

Right now, in your hands, you hold the most powerful tool humanity has ever created: artificial intelligence. Use it. Speak your ideas. Refine them. Then build action plans to bring them to life. Whatever your skill set design, writing, coding, teaching, organizing this is your time to manifest your vision.

We now have the ability to build an alternative: a **Sovereign Decentralized Network**. A parallel digital world that needs *human beings*, not just machines. A new economy. A new infrastructure. A **real-life digital Zion**, like in

The Matrix, where we don't just survive, we thrive on our own terms.

Just like the last human stronghold in the movie, this isn't about fighting machines with fists, it's about *out-creating* them. We're talking about communities powered by mesh networks, encrypted by design, and fueled by peer-to-peer economies. It's a world where creativity, connection, and sovereignty take center stage.

We even have the choice to use **alternative AI tools** ones that align with our values.

Take **Venice**, for example. Developed by Erik Voorhees, one of the original pioneers of the Bitcoin movement, Venice (listed as **VVV** on Crypto Market Cap) empowers users to build AI applications whether for image generation or deep-thinking models while honoring the principles of privacy and decentralization.

On the **Start9 Marketplace**, tools like **Stable Diffusion** bring creative control back to the user. This generative model can craft original images from text prompts or modify existing ones similar in concept to MidJourney or DALL·E 2, but fully self-hosted and private.

Then there's **FreeGPT-2**, which combines the backend power of **Ollama** (for running large language models locally) with the clean, intuitive interface of **Open WebUI**. This setup lets you run your own GPT style assistant completely offline, with no data leakage and no gatekeepers.

And when you're ready to level up, the path is open to train your own **custom AI models**, tailored to your exact needs whether for development, research, security, or creative expression.

The sky? That's no longer the limit. It's just the beginning.

Here's How You Can Get Started

Build Inside the CJDNS (Hyperboria) Network

Set up mesh nodes and contribute to a privacy-first, IP address-free internet powered by cryptographic trust.

Host Open-Source SaaS Replacements

Set up decentralized clones of popular tools using platforms like:

1. **Nextcloud** - File storage and collaboration
2. **CryptPad** - Encrypted document editing
3. **Funkwhale** - Decentralized music streaming
4. **PeerTube** - Decentralized video platform
5. **Matrix / Element** - Encrypted, decentralized chat
6. **Ghost / WriteFreely** - For sovereign, independent publishing
7. **Venice** - Privacy-first AI application platform
8. **Stable Diffusion** - Self-hosted image generation
9. **FreeGPT-2** - Fully local GPT model for private AI conversations

Develop and Use Bitcoin/Lightning-Powered Services

Accept Lightning payments using BTCPay Server, run your own node, or sell digital goods with microtransactions.

Create Your Own Micro-Communities

Host newsletters, forums, or stores with open-source tools. Invite people you trust and build something resilient.

Host Your Own Infrastructure with Start9 or Umbrel

Run your own email, password manager, Git repo, AI models, media library, and more fully sovereign and independent of Big Tech.

This isn't just about rebellion, it's about creation. We're not fighting the future we're building one of our own designs. One that honors privacy, autonomy, and community.

You are not obsolete. You are the one laying bricks in the new digital city.

Welcome to the Sovereign Era.

The Vision Questions: How can like-minded free human beings create a better world where we have total control of our purchasing power? A place where we can buy and sell with one another ethical goods and services? How do we build a business-to-business network that filters out exploitation? How do we build a platform that stops slave labor products? How do we really protect the destruction of natural resources like the Amazon and our atmosphere?

SECRET #39: The Solution That Started in a Coding Bootcamp

From 18-Wheeler to Web 3.0 Revolutionary

After the creation of Bitcoin way back in 2009 and that curious criminal marketplace called Silk Road, the solution presented itself: What if we built honest, open-source, open-access ethical marketplaces that have the same security as major corporate institutions? What if Bitcoin was able to transact like a credit card, and we could buy and sell with alternative currency?

Fast forward to 2016 in Pearland, Texas, after a short stint driving an 18-wheeler semi. I was able to go back to the joy of programming. While driving state to state, I found a 9-week coding bootcamp called Coder Camps, and there I learned how to be a better coder. I enjoyed the experience and completed it twice one because I really do enjoy it, and two because I needed a place to stay.

After completion of the course, for my final project, I decided to see how close I could come to the Bit Main Street vision. For our graduation project, I asked my co-students if we could build that vision, and in just a few weeks, Bit Main Street was born. At the time, blockchain development wasn't even a thought, but I understood the need. So the team completed and unveiled the project. I experienced the joy of the Law of Attraction. Now, ten years later, that vision has become a reality.

Web 3.0 Service Provider Framework

The Technical Foundation of Freedom

The concept of Web 3.0 service providers represents the next evolution in decentralized infrastructure. These entities provide essential decentralized tools and services while maintaining the principles of user sovereignty and privacy like (DSN).

Key Components of the Light Web:

Decentralized hosting solutions: IPFS, Filecoin, and NextCloud alternatives

Crypto-native payment systems: Lightning Network, Bitcoin, and DeFi integration

Privacy-preserving communication tools: Tor-based messaging and encrypted channels

Censorship-resistant marketplaces: Peer-to-peer trading without intermediaries

How This Works: If you live in the land of the free, wouldn't you like tools to help you maintain that freedom? Tools that allow you to trade goods and services? Tools that allow you to build a place to speak your peace freely? These are necessities. What I am offering is the knowledge and tools on how to do just that. We leverage the security of the blockchain and the power of cryptocurrency by building communities where we can thrive. This is what we call Decentralized Sovereign Networks (DSN)

Building Your Decentralized Infrastructure Empire

Technical Requirements for Your Light Web Business:

Raspberry Pi or similar hardware for node operation

Reliable internet connectivity for 24/7 operations

Basic networking knowledge (I'll teach you everything you need)

Security best practices implementation following our Bitcoin-Ethereum security model

Service Offerings That Generate Income:

Lightning Network Node Operation:

RoboSats: A simple and private Lightning P2P exchange where you can arbitrage BTC using Tor

LNbits: Lightning Network dashboard with numerous Bitcoin apps start your own Lightning business and earn BTC

Ride The Lightning (RTL): A sleek, browser-based interface to manage your Lightning node with ease track payments, manage channels, and monitor your network

Alby Hub: A browser extension that integrates Lightning payments directly into your web experience great for tipping, streaming sats, or integrating with Web 3.0 apps

BTCPay Server: A self-hosted, open-source Bitcoin and Lightning payment processor accept payments directly into your wallet with no third parties or fees

IPFS and Satoshi For Storage Services:

IPFS Podcasting: Earn Bitcoin by running an IPFS podcasting node

Satoshi For Storage: Host encrypted, time-limited files using your node users pay in Bitcoin via Lightning for temporary access

NextCloud Hosting: Build personal cloud storage devices or host files for businesses like websites

Decentralized Marketplace Development:

Build marketplaces and host secure products for people

Sell your skills as a developer on decentralized platforms

Create ethical alternatives to exploitative centralized platforms

DeFi Jedi Crypto Academy: Your Real World Training Path

Current Course Curriculum – As Offered on Our Platform

The Fundamentals:

What is Cryptocurrency? (7:45)

What is Blockchain Technology? (12:07)

Core Concepts:

What is DeFi? (31:13)

Web3: The Decentralized Internet of the Future Explained (14:37)

Web 3.0 Tools and Fundamentals:

The Interplanetary File System (IPFS) Explained (12:07)

What is the Non-Fungible Token (NFT)? (10:55)

What is Staking in Crypto? (16:32)

What Are Decentralized Exchanges (DEXs)? (18:41)

Initial Coin Offering Explained (20:16)

Strike and the Lightning Network (6:09)

Onboarding & How-To Guides:

Wallets and Applications: Setup and Use

The Great Offer:

What is a Web 3.0 Service Provider?

Bonus Session:

The Power of Cryptocurrency – Questions and Answers

The Three-Tier Opportunity Structure

Offer 1: The Power of Cryptocurrency Newsletter - $5/month

Access to a growing library of crypto knowledge

Limited access to the Bit Main Street Network

Special offers and discounts for new members

Includes a 7-day free trial

Offer 2: DeFi Web 3.0 Fundamental Special - $30/month

Full access to the DeFi Jedi Crypto Academy

* One free Web 3.0 consultation session (limited offer)

Full access to the Bit Main Street Network

Unlocking the Secrets digital download

Full access to newsletter content

Includes a 7-day free trial

Offer 3: Mastermind Membership & Web 3.0 Entrepreneur Services - $124.99/month

Web 3.0 service provider opportunities

Payment service and website setup

Access to exclusive crypto products

Full access to the entrepreneur marketplace

Private access to mastermind live meetings

* Pre-qualification required to join (exclusive offer)

The Vision Realized: Bit Main Street Farm

Beyond Digital Creating Physical Freedom

"In a world guided by Ubuntu, we rise together not by taking more, but by creating value that multiplies. This is not a zero-sum hustle; it's a 360° exchange of energy, equity, and elevation where every deal uplifts the circle, not just the center."

The Sovereign Network isn't just about technology it's about reclaiming every dimension of freedom. While most are focused on escaping digital surveillance, we're building something deeper: a way to live clean, connected, and in control. That's why I decided to create a real-world anchor for our decentralized movement.

Bit Main Street Farm is that anchor a physical space where like-minded thinkers and doers can come together and build. Not just online but in real life. A place to grow our own organic food free from GMOs and chemicals. A space to cultivate healing herbs, rare seeds, raw honey, and the future we've all been dreaming of.

To build this vision, I'm offering access to a limited amount of land only to those who are members of the Network. It starts with those who are ready. To qualify, you must be a member of the DeFi Jedi Mastermind Group. Why? Because this isn't just about farming it's about alignment. Vision. Purpose. And a shared commitment to sovereignty. For details meet me on the DeFi Jedi weekly video conference call.

As a Mastermind member, you'll have access to the farm to nourish your family, contribute to the mission, and witness what's possible when vision becomes action. Join us and be part of something sacred, sustainable, and unstoppable. Keep in mind space is limited

The Call to Adventure

Your Legend of Zelda Moment

What I am offering you is not just education or business opportunities, it's a complete transformation from the dying fiat system to a sovereign, decentralized future. When you become a member, you will learn how to build your own Decentralized Sovereign Network. I will teach you personally. You will have access to services that you will learn how to set up. Then you can become your own Web 3.0 Service Provider or set up your current business as an alternative to the fiat system.

If our minds are truly connected, you will see the massive opportunity of prosperity.

This information was not available to the public because of restrictions imposed by the powers that should not be. But now, with the 2025 regulatory renaissance, we can finally build the ethical, decentralized economy we've always envisioned.

The choice is yours: Continue playing by the old rules of the fiat system, or join us in building the Light Web, a place where freedom, honesty, and prosperity can flourish together.

Thank you for taking the time to read this and having faith in me to guide you on this new venture, because I do this in honor of Amenkara, my mentor. "I owe you love is the way."

Chapter 10

Step-by-Step DeFi Setup Guide - Your Complete 2028 Implementation Roadmap

"The journey of a thousand miles begins with a single step. In DeFi, that step is setting up your secure infrastructure."

After learning about Web 3.0 foundations, regulatory landscapes, and advanced strategies, it's time for implementation. This chapter provides the exact step-by-step process to get you operational in DeFi by 2028, with current best practices and security protocols.

What You'll Accomplish:

Set up secure wallet infrastructure (hot, cold, and Lightning)

Execute your first DeFi transactions safely

Implement military-grade security protocols

Connect to major DeFi platforms with confidence

Create a scalable system for 2028 opportunities

SECRET #40: The Three-Wallet Security Architecture

Why Single Wallets Are a Security Disaster

Most DeFi users make a critical mistake: they use one wallet for everything. This is like keeping all your money in your back pocket while walking through a dangerous neighborhood. Professional DeFi users implement a three-wallet architecture that protects wealth while enabling opportunity.

The Professional Wallet Structure:

> **Cold Storage Vault (80-90% of holdings): Hardware wallet for long-term storage**
>
> **DeFi Operating Wallet (5-15% of holdings): Software wallet for active protocols**
>
> **Lightning Network Wallet (1-5% of holdings): For Bitcoin transactions and payments**

This architecture ensures that even if your operating wallet is compromised, your wealth remains secure while you maintain full DeFi functionality.

Phase 1: Cold Storage Setup - Your Digital Vault

Hardware Wallet Selection and Setup

Ledger Setup (Recommended for Beginners):

Step 1: Purchase and Verify

1. Buy directly from ledger.com (never from third parties)
2. Verify packaging seal is intact
3. Ensure no pre-written recovery phrases are included
4. Check device authenticity through Ledger Live app

Step 2: Initial Configuration

1. Download Ledger Live from official website
2. Connect device and follow setup wizard
3. Generate new 24-word recovery phrase (never use a pre-made one)
4. Write recovery phrases on provided cards (never digital storage)
5. Verify recovery phrases by entering words in random order
6. Set strong PIN (never use birthdays or obvious numbers)

Trezor Setup (Advanced Security Features):

Enhanced Security Protocol:

1. Purchase from trezor.io official store
2. Verify holographic seals and packaging
3. Use Trezor Suite for setup (download from official site only)
4. Enable passphrase protection for additional security layer
5. Create multiple hidden wallets using different passphrases
6. Test recovery process with small amounts before large transfers

Recovery Phrase Security Protocol

SECRET #41: The Steganographic Backup Method

How Professionals Hide Recovery Phrases

Never store your 24-word recovery phrase in plain text. Professional crypto users employ steganographic methods to hide their phrases in plain sight:

> **Book Method:** Mark specific words in a book, with your seed words corresponding to marked positions

Photo Method: Hide word positions in photo metadata or use specific objects in photos to represent word order

Metal Backup: Use titanium plates (fire/water resistant) with word positions etched

Geographic Distribution: Split phrases across multiple secure locations

Never Do: Email phrases to yourself, store in cloud services, take photos of phrases, or keep them in password managers.

Phase 2: DeFi Operating Wallet Setup

MetaMask Professional Configuration

Step 1: Secure Installation

1. Download only from metamask.io
2. Verify browser extension authenticity (check developer signatures)
3. Create new wallet (never import existing phrases)

4. Generate fresh 12-word recovery phrase
5. Fund only with small amounts initially (test transactions)

Step 2: Network Configuration

Add Polygon Network:

Network Name: Polygon Mainnet

RPC URL: https://polygon-rpc.com

Chain ID: 137

Currency Symbol: MATIC

Block Explorer: https://polygonscan.com

Add Arbitrum Network:

Network Name: Arbitrum One

RPC URL: https://arb1.arbitrum.io/rpc

Chain ID: 42161

Currency Symbol: ETH

Block Explorer: https://arbiscan.io

Add Optimism Network:

Network Name: Optimism

RPC URL: https://mainnet.optimism.io

Chain ID: 10

Currency Symbol: ETH

Block Explorer: https://optimistic.etherscan.io

Exodus Wallet Setup (User-Friendly Alternative)

Exodus Configuration for DeFi:

1. Download from exodus.com (desktop version recommended)
2. Create new wallet with strong password
3. Enable built-in DeFi features (Compound, Aave integration)
4. Configure portfolio tracking for yield farming positions
5. Set up built-in exchange for easy swaps
6. Export private keys to hardware wallet for additional security

Phase 3: Lightning Network Wallet Setup

Phoenix Wallet (Beginner-Friendly)

Phoenix Lightning Setup:

1. Download Phoenix from official app stores or phoenix.acinq.co
2. Create new wallet (automatic channel management)
3. Fund with small Bitcoin amount for testing
4. Practice instant payments with test transactions
5. Enable automatic channel rebalancing

Blue Wallet (Advanced Features)

Blue Wallet Professional Setup:

1. Download from www.bluewallet.io
2. Create separate Bitcoin and Lightning wallets
3. Import watch-only wallet from hardware device
4. Configure custom Lightning node connection (optional)
5. Set up LNURL for easy receiving
6. Enable Tor for enhanced privacy

SECRET #42: Lightning Network Arbitrage Opportunities

How to Profit from Lightning Network Infrastructure

Professional Lightning users don't just use the network—they profit from it. Here's how:

- **Channel Liquidity Provision:** Run Lightning nodes and earn routing fees
- **Cross-Exchange Arbitrage:** Use Lightning for instant Bitcoin transfers between exchanges
- **Circular Rebalancing:** Earn fees by rebalancing channels for other node operators
- **Lightning Services:** Offer Lightning-based services (payments, streaming, gaming)

With regulatory clarity and institutional adoption coming, Lightning Network usage will explode by 2028, creating significant revenue opportunities for early infrastructure providers.

Phase 4: Your First DeFi Transactions

Test Transaction Protocol

Safe First Steps (Use Small Amounts):

1. Ethereum Mainnet Test:

- Send $10 worth of ETH from exchange to MetaMask
- Verify transaction on www.etherscan.io
- Practice sending ETH back to exchange
- Check gas fees and optimize timing

2. Polygon Test:

- Bridge $20 worth of ETH to Polygon using official bridge
- Experience Layer 2 speed and low fees
- Test swap on QuickSwap or SushiSwap
- Bridge back to Ethereum mainnet

3. Lightning Test:

- Fund Lightning wallet with $5 worth of Bitcoin
- Make instant payment to Lightning address
- Receive Lightning payment from friend/service

- Close channel and return to on-chain Bitcoin

First DeFi Protocol Interaction

Aave Lending Test (Polygon Network):

1. Visit app.aave.com
2. Connect MetaMask wallet
3. Switch to Polygon network
4. Supply $25 worth of USDC to earn interest
5. Monitor earning accumulation for 24 hours
6. Withdraw funds plus earned interest
7. Verify transaction success on PolygonScan

Uniswap Swap Test (Ethereum Mainnet):

1. Visit app.uniswap.org
2. Connect MetaMask wallet
3. Swap $20 worth of ETH for USDC
4. Review gas fees before confirming
5. Execute transaction and wait for confirmation
6. Swap USDC back to ETH (understanding slippage)
7. Calculate total cost including gas fees

Phase 5: Security Implementation

SECRET #43: The Operational Security Checklist

Military-Grade DeFi Security Protocol

Daily Operations Security:

- **Browser Hygiene:** Use dedicated browser for DeFi (Firefox with strict settings)
- **URL Verification:** Bookmark official sites, never click links in Discord/Telegram
- **Contract Verification:** Always verify contract addresses on multiple sources
- **Transaction Simulation:** Use Tenderly to simulate complex transactions
- **Gas Optimization:** Use ETH Gas Station for optimal fee timing

Weekly Security Maintenance:

- Review all wallet transactions for unauthorized activity
- Update wallet software to latest versions

- Check token approvals and revoke unnecessary permissions
- Verify hardware wallet firmware is current
- Backup any new wallet data or configurations

Monthly Security Audit:

- Test hardware wallet recovery process with small amounts
- Review and update emergency recovery procedures
- Assess protocol risks and adjust position sizes
- Update security software and operating systems
- Review portfolio allocation and rebalance if necessary

Advanced Security Measures

Multi-Signature Setup (For Large Holdings):

1. Use Gnosis Safe for multi-sig wallet creation

2. Set up 2-of-3 or 3-of-5 signature requirements
3. Distribute signing keys across multiple hardware wallets
4. Store wallets in geographically separate locations
5. Test multi-sig functionality with small transactions
6. Document recovery procedures for all signers

Phase 6: Scaling for 2028 Opportunities

Infrastructure Preparation

2028-Ready Configuration:

- **Multiple Exchange Accounts:** Set up accounts on 3-5 major exchanges for liquidity
- **Cross-Chain Capabilities:** Configure wallets for all major networks (Ethereum, Polygon, Arbitrum, Optimism, BSC)

- **Institutional Readiness:** Prepare for higher capital limits and compliance requirements
- **Automated Tools:** Set up DeFi Pulse, DeBank, and Zapper for portfolio tracking
- **Tax Documentation:** Use CoinTracker or similar for automated tax reporting

SECRET #44: The 2028 Scaling Strategy

Preparing for Institutional DeFi Adoption

By 2028, DeFi will handle institutional-level capital flows. Prepare now:

- **Compliance Infrastructure:** Document all transactions for regulatory reporting
- **Professional Tools:** Use institutional-grade analytics and risk management platforms
- **Network Diversification:** Spread operations across multiple Layer 1 and Layer 2 networks

- **Liquidity Partnerships:** Establish relationships with market makers and OTC desks
- **Insurance Coverage:** Protect large positions with DeFi insurance protocols

Those who build professional-grade infrastructure now will capture disproportionate value when institutional money floods into DeFi.

Emergency Procedures and Recovery

Emergency Action Plan:

- **Wallet Compromise:** Immediately transfer funds to backup hardware wallet
- **Protocol Exploit:** Exit positions and document losses for insurance/tax purposes
- **Regulatory Changes:** Have exit strategies for multiple jurisdictions
- **Technical Failures:** Maintain backup access methods for all platforms

- **Personal Emergency:** Ensure trusted person can access recovery information

Your DeFi Success Checklist

Phase 1 Complete ✓

Hardware wallet purchased and configured

Recovery phrase secured using steganographic method

Cold storage tested with small transactions

Phase 2 Complete ✓

MetaMask or Exodus wallet set up

Multiple networks configured (Polygon, Arbitrum, Optimism)

Operating wallet funded with appropriate amounts

Phase 3 Complete ✓

Lightning wallet installed and tested

Instant Bitcoin payments verified

Lightning arbitrage opportunities identified

Phase 4 Complete ✓

First DeFi transactions executed successfully

Gas optimization strategies implemented

Protocol interactions documented and understood

Phase 5 Complete ✓

Security protocols implemented and tested

Emergency procedures documented

Regular security maintenance scheduled

Phase 6 Complete ✓

Infrastructure scaled for institutional adoption

2028 positioning strategies activated

Professional-grade tools and partnerships established

Congratulations! You now have the complete technical infrastructure to participate in the DeFi revolution safely and profitably. Your setup is ready for the 2028 Bitcoin halving catalyst and the institutional adoption wave that will follow.

Remember: Start small, test everything, and scale gradually. The infrastructure you build today will determine your success when the next crypto Supercycle arrives.

BONUS SECTION

Special Edition Reference Materials

"Knowledge is the ultimate currency in the DeFi revolution. These bonus materials ensure you're always equipped with the insights that matter."

Congratulations! As a reader of the Special Edition of "Unlocking the Secrets of Web 3.0 Wealth," you now have access to exclusive bonus materials that complement your journey to 2028 financial freedom.

Your Special Edition Includes:

Complete DeFi Glossary: 200+ essential terms with risk assessments and 2028 strategic focus

Quick Reference Guides: Formulas, acronyms, and protocol comparisons

Strategic Terminology: Future-focused definitions for institutional adoption

Security Reference: Complete safety terminology and best practices

These materials are designed to serve as your permanent reference guide bookmark this section and return to it as you implement the strategies outlined in the previous chapters. Master the language, master the technology, master your financial future.

Complete DeFi Glossary

Your A-Z Guide to Decentralized Finance

"In the world of DeFi, knowledge of the language is power. Master the terms, master the technology."

This comprehensive glossary contains over 200 essential DeFi terms, concepts, and protocols. Whether you're a beginner learning the basics or an advanced user looking for precise definitions, this reference guide will serve as your go-to resource for navigating the complex world of decentralized finance.

How to Use This Glossary:

Cross-References: Terms in *italics* link to other definitions in this glossary

Risk Indicators: High Risk | Medium Risk | Low Risk

2028 Relevance: Critical for 2028 positioning

Practical Examples: Real-world usage scenarios included where applicable

A

Aave (AAVE) - Low Risk | Critical for 2028

A leading decentralized lending protocol that allows users to lend and borrow cryptocurrencies without intermediaries. Features include *flash loans*, credit delegation, and yield farming opportunities. Aave operates on multiple networks including Ethereum, Polygon, and Avalanche.

Example: Supply USDC to Aave on Polygon network to earn 8-15% APY while maintaining the ability to withdraw instantly.

Address - Low Risk

A unique identifier on a blockchain, similar to a bank account number, used to send and receive cryptocurrency. Ethereum addresses start with "0x" followed by 40 hexadecimal characters.

Example:
0x742d35Cc6634Bc532d78b96b8f73ae19aa8C0a55

Aggregator - Low Risk

A platform that combines liquidity from multiple *decentralized exchanges (DEXs)* to find the best prices for token swaps. Popular aggregators include *1inch* and Matcha.

Alpha - Medium Risk | Critical for 2028

Exclusive, early-stage investment opportunities or information that can generate superior returns. In DeFi, "alpha" often refers to new protocols, token launches, or yield farming strategies before they become widely known.

AMM (Automated Market Maker) - Low Risk | Critical for 2028

A type of *decentralized exchange* that uses mathematical formulas and liquidity pools instead of traditional order books to determine asset prices. *Uniswap* and *SushiSwap* are popular AMMs.

Key Formula: $x * y = k$ (constant product formula used by Uniswap)

Annual Percentage Yield (APY) - Low Risk

The real rate of return earned on an investment, taking into account the effect of compounding interest. In DeFi, APY shows how much you can earn from *yield farming*, *staking*, or *liquidity provision*.

Example: A 100% APY means your investment doubles in one year with compounding.

Arbitrage - Medium Risk | Critical for 2028

The practice of buying an asset on one exchange and selling it on another to profit from price differences. *Flash loans* enable instant arbitrage without requiring initial capital.

Audit - Low Risk

A security review of smart contract code performed by specialized firms to identify vulnerabilities and bugs. Always check if a protocol has been audited by reputable firms like ConsenSys, Trail of Bits, or OpenZeppelin.

B

Balancer (BAL) - Low Risk

An automated portfolio manager and *decentralized exchange* that allows users to create custom liquidity pools with multiple tokens and different weightings.

Bitcoin (BTC) - Low Risk | Critical for 2028

The first and most secure cryptocurrency, often used as a store of value in DeFi through *wrapped* versions like *WBTC*. Essential for 2028 positioning due to the *halving event.*

Block - Low Risk

A collection of transactions grouped together and added to the blockchain. Each block contains a timestamp, transaction data, and a reference to the previous block.

Blockchain - Low Risk | Critical for 2028

A distributed ledger technology that maintains a continuously growing list of records (blocks) linked and secured using cryptography. The foundation of all DeFi protocols.

Bridge - Medium Risk

Infrastructure that enables the transfer of tokens and data between different blockchains. Examples include the Polygon Bridge and Arbitrum Bridge. Bridges carry smart contract risk.

Bull Market - Low Risk | Critical for 2028

A period of rising cryptocurrency prices and investor optimism. The 2028 *Bitcoin halving* is expected to trigger the next major bull market.

Burn - Low Risk

The permanent removal of tokens from circulation, typically to reduce supply and increase scarcity. Many DeFi protocols burn tokens as part of their tokenomics.

C

CEX (Centralized Exchange) - Medium Risk

Traditional cryptocurrency exchanges like Coinbase, Binance, or Kraken that are controlled by a central authority. Contrasts with *DEX (Decentralized Exchange)*.

Clearnet - Medium Risk

The publicly accessible portion of the internet that operates through traditional domain names (like .com, .org) and is indexed by search engines. Unlike the dark web or private networks, Clearnet traffic is typically unencrypted and routed through centralized infrastructure, making it more vulnerable to surveillance and censorship.

CJDNS (Caleb James Delisle Network Suite) - Low Risk

An open-source networking protocol that uses public key cryptography to assign IPv6 addresses and enable encrypted, trustless communication between peers. CJDNS is the foundation of mesh networks like Hyperboria, designed to create a secure, decentralized internet without centralized routing authorities.

Cold Storage - Low Risk

Storing cryptocurrency offline in hardware wallets or paper wallets to protect against hacking. Essential for the *three-wallet security architecture* outlined in Chapter 10.

Collateral - Low Risk

Assets pledged as security for a loan. In DeFi lending, you must provide collateral worth more than the loan amount to protect against default risk.

Example: Deposit $150 worth of ETH to borrow $100 worth of USDC (150% collateralization ratio).

Compound (COMP) - Low Risk | Critical for 2028

A pioneering DeFi lending protocol that introduced algorithmic interest rates and *cTokens*. Users earn interest on supplied assets and can borrow against them.

Composability - Low Risk | Critical for 2028

The ability to combine different DeFi protocols like building blocks to create new financial products. Often called "money legos" due to this modular nature.

Consensus Mechanism - Low Risk

The method by which a blockchain network agrees on the validity of transactions. *Proof of Work* (Bitcoin) and *Proof of Stake* (Ethereum 2.0) are common mechanisms.

Curve Finance (CRV) - Low Risk

A decentralized exchange optimized for *stablecoin* trading with low slippage. Popular for earning yields on stablecoin pairs.

Custody - Low Risk

Control over cryptocurrency private keys. "Self-custody" means you control your own keys, while "custodial" means a third party controls them.

D

DAO (Decentralized Autonomous Organization) - Low Risk | Critical for 2028

An organization governed by smart contracts and token holders rather than traditional management. Members vote on proposals using *governance tokens.*

dApp (Decentralized Application) - Low Risk | Critical for 2028

Applications built on blockchain networks that operate without central control. Examples include *Uniswap, Aave,* and *Compound.*

DeFi (Decentralized Finance) - Low Risk | Critical for 2028

A movement to recreate traditional financial systems using blockchain technology, eliminating intermediaries and enabling global, permissionless access to financial services.

Degen (Short for Degenerate Trader) - High Risk | Critical for 2028

A slang term in crypto culture referring to risk-loving, often highly experienced traders who dive deep into speculative assets, DeFi protocols, and early-stage projects. While the term began as a joke, many "Degens" are skilled, battle-tested investors who thrive in high-volatility environments and often discover opportunities before the mainstream.

DePin (Decentralized Physical Infrastructure Network) - Medium Risk | Emerging Sector for 2028

A growing movement focused on building real-world infrastructure such as wireless networks, energy grids, and sensor systems using blockchain-based incentives and decentralized governance instead of centralized ownership models.

DEX (Decentralized Exchange) - Low Risk | Critical for 2028

Cryptocurrency exchanges that operate without central authority, allowing peer-to-peer trading through *smart contracts*. Examples: *Uniswap*, *SushiSwap*, *PancakeSwap*.

Diamond Hands - Low Risk

Slang for holding cryptocurrency investments for long periods despite market volatility. Opposite of *paper hands*.

Double Spending - Low Risk

The risk of spending the same cryptocurrency twice. Blockchain consensus mechanisms prevent this attack.

DRS (Decentralized Reputation System) - Medium Risk

Systems that track user behavior and reliability in DeFi protocols to enable trust without central authorities.

E

EIP (Ethereum Improvement Proposal) - Low Risk

Technical documents that propose changes to the Ethereum network. EIP-1559 introduced fee burning, while EIP-4844 will reduce Layer 2 costs.

ERC-20 - Low Risk

The technical standard for fungible tokens on Ethereum. Most DeFi tokens follow this standard, enabling interoperability between protocols.

Ethereum (ETH) - Low Risk | Critical for 2028

The leading smart contract platform that hosts most DeFi protocols. Essential for 2028 DeFi strategies due to its programmability and ecosystem.

EVM (Ethereum Virtual Machine) - Medium Risk

The runtime environment for smart contracts on Ethereum. Many other blockchains are "EVM-compatible," allowing them to run Ethereum applications.

Exchange Rate - Low Risk

The price of one cryptocurrency relative to another. DeFi protocols use *oracles* to determine accurate exchange rates.

F

Fiat - Low Risk

Government-issued currency like USD, EUR, or JPY. DeFi aims to reduce dependence on fiat currencies through decentralized alternatives.

Flash Loan - Medium Risk | Critical for 2028

Uncollateralized loans that must be borrowed and repaid within a single transaction. Enables *arbitrage* and complex DeFi strategies without initial capital.

Risk: Requires technical knowledge to execute safely.

FOMO (Fear of Missing Out) - Medium Risk

The anxiety that drives impulsive investment decisions. Can lead to buying at market tops or investing in risky protocols without proper research.

Fork - Low Risk

A change to blockchain rules. "Hard forks" create new blockchains (like Bitcoin Cash), while "soft forks" are backward-compatible upgrades.

FUD (Fear, Uncertainty, Doubt) - Low Risk

Negative sentiment spread about cryptocurrencies or protocols, often used to manipulate prices or discourage adoption.

G

Gas - Medium Risk

The fee required to execute transactions on Ethereum, paid in *gwei*. Higher gas fees result in faster transaction processing but increase costs.

Optimization: Use Layer 2 solutions like Polygon or Arbitrum for lower gas fees.

Governance Token - Low Risk | Critical for 2028

Tokens that give holders voting rights in protocol decisions. Examples include UNI (Uniswap), AAVE (Aave), and COMP (Compound).

Gwei - Low Risk

A denomination of Ethereum, where 1 ETH = 1 billion gwei. Gas prices are typically measured in gwei.

H

Halving - Low Risk | Critical for 2028

An event that occurs approximately every four years where Bitcoin's block reward is cut in half, reducing new supply. The 2028 halving is expected to trigger massive price appreciation.

Hardware Wallet - Low Risk

Physical devices that store cryptocurrency private keys offline for maximum security. Essential component of the *three-wallet security architecture*.

Hash - Low Risk

A fixed-length string generated by a mathematical function that uniquely identifies data. Used extensively in blockchain for security and verification.

HODL - Low Risk

Originally a misspelling of "hold," now a popular strategy of buying and holding cryptocurrency long-term regardless of price volatility.

Hot Wallet - Medium Risk

Cryptocurrency wallets connected to the internet, used for frequent transactions. More convenient but less secure than *cold storage*.

Hyperboria Mesh Network - Low Risk

A decentralized, encrypted mesh network built using CJDNS (Cjdns). Hyperboria enables peer-to-peer communication over IPv6, forming a global, community-owned internet where every node routes traffic securely without relying on traditional ISPs or centralized infrastructure.

Impermanent Loss - Medium Risk | Critical for 2028

The temporary loss in value experienced when providing liquidity to *AMMs* due to price changes between deposited tokens. Can become permanent if not managed properly.

Mitigation: Provide liquidity to correlated pairs like ETH/stETH or use delta-neutral strategies.

Index Token - Low Risk

Tokens that represent a basket of other cryptocurrencies, providing diversified exposure. Examples include DPI (DeFi Pulse Index) and BED (Bankless BED Index).

Infinity Approval - High Risk

Granting unlimited spending permission to smart contracts. Convenient but risky if the contract is compromised. Regularly revoke unnecessary approvals.

Interoperability - Low Risk | Critical for 2028

The ability of different blockchains to communicate and transfer value. Critical for 2028 DeFi strategies that span multiple networks.

IPFS (Inter-Planetary File System) Low Risk

A decentralized storage network used by many DeFi protocols to store metadata and ensure censorship resistance.

J

Junk Bond - High Risk

High-risk, high-yield debt securities. In DeFi, protocols offering extremely high APYs (>100%) often carry similar risks.

K

KYC (Know Your Customer) - Medium Risk

Identity verification requirements imposed by centralized exchanges and some DeFi protocols. True decentralized protocols operate without KYC.

L

Layer 1 - Low Risk | Critical for 2028

Base blockchain networks like Bitcoin, Ethereum, and Solana. The foundation layer where smart contracts and transactions are settled.

Layer 2 - Low Risk | Critical for 2028

Scaling solutions built on top of Layer 1 blockchains to reduce fees and increase transaction speed. Examples: Polygon, Arbitrum, Optimism.

Lightning Network - Low Risk | Critical for 2028

Bitcoin's Layer 2 solution enabling instant, low-cost payments. Essential for 2028 Bitcoin adoption and *arbitrage opportunities*.

Liquidity - Low Risk | Critical for 2028

The ease with which an asset can be bought or sold without affecting its price. Deep liquidity enables large trades with minimal *slippage*.

Liquidity Mining - Low Risk | Critical for 2028

Earning token rewards by providing liquidity to DeFi protocols. A key strategy for maximizing yields in the 2028 DeFi ecosystem.

Liquidity Pool - Low Risk | Critical for 2028

Smart contracts containing tokens that enable trading on *DEXs*. Liquidity providers earn fees from trades that occur in their pools.

Liquidation - Medium Risk

The automatic sale of collateral when its value falls below the required threshold for a loan. Can result in significant losses if not monitored.

M

MakerDAO (MKR) - Low Risk | Critical for 2028

The protocol behind the DAI stablecoin, governed by MKR token holders. Pioneered decentralized governance and overcollateralized stablecoins.

Mempool - Low Risk

The pool of unconfirmed transactions waiting to be processed by miners or validators. Understanding mempool dynamics helps optimize gas fees.

MetaMask - Low Risk

The most popular Ethereum wallet browser extension, essential for interacting with DeFi protocols. Part of the *DeFi operating wallet* setup.

MEV (Maximal Extractable Value) - Medium Risk

Profit extracted by miners or validators through transaction ordering, arbitrage, and front-running. Can impact regular users through higher slippage.

Multi-Sig - Low Risk

Wallets requiring multiple signatures to authorize transactions, providing enhanced security for large holdings. Essential for institutional DeFi operations.

N

NFT (Non-Fungible Token) - Medium Risk

Unique digital assets representing ownership of specific items. While not directly DeFi, NFTs can be used as *collateral* in some lending protocols.

Node - Low Risk

Computers that maintain copies of blockchain data and validate transactions. Running nodes supports network decentralization and security.

Nonce - Low Risk

A number used once in cryptographic communication, preventing replay attacks. In Ethereum, it tracks the number of transactions sent from an address.

O

Oracle - Low Risk | Critical for 2028

Services that provide external data to smart contracts, such as price feeds. *Chainlink* is the leading oracle network. Critical for DeFi protocol security.

Order Book - Low Risk

Traditional exchange system listing buy and sell orders. DEXs like *dYdX* use order books, while *AMMs* use liquidity pools instead.

OTC (Over-the-Counter) - Medium Risk

Direct trading between parties without using exchanges. Common for large transactions to avoid market impact and slippage.

P

Paper Hands - Medium Risk

Slang for selling investments quickly due to fear or panic. Opposite of *diamond hands*. Often results in losses during volatile periods.

Permissionless - Low Risk | Critical for 2028

Systems that allow anyone to participate without approval from central authorities. A core principle of DeFi that enables global financial inclusion.

Private Key - Low Risk

A secret cryptographic key that proves ownership of a cryptocurrency address. "Not your keys, not your crypto" emphasizes the importance of self-custody.

Protocol - Low Risk | Critical for 2028

A set of rules and standards that define how a blockchain network or DeFi application operates. Examples include HTTP for web and smart contracts for DeFi.

Proof of Stake (PoS) - Low Risk

A consensus mechanism where validators are chosen to create new blocks based on their stake in the network. Used by Ethereum 2.0 and many other blockchains.

Proof of Work (PoW) - Low Risk

A consensus mechanism where miners compete to solve cryptographic puzzles to create new blocks. Used by Bitcoin and provides the highest security.

Q

QR Code - Low Risk

Two-dimensional barcodes that encode cryptocurrency addresses, making it easier to send transactions without typing long addresses.

R

Raspberry Pi - Low Risk

A low-cost, credit card-sized computer designed for education, experimentation, and innovation. In the Web 3.0 world, it's often used to run Bitcoin nodes, mesh networks, or personal servers like Start9 giving individuals the power to build decentralized systems from the ground up.

Reentrancy Attack - High Risk

A smart contract vulnerability where external calls can be made before state changes are finalized. The 2016 DAO hack used this exploit.

Rug Pull - High Risk

A scam where developers abandon a project and steal investor funds. Always verify protocol audits and team credibility before investing.

S

Satoshi (SAT) - Low Risk

The smallest unit of Bitcoin, named after its mysterious creator, Satoshi Nakamoto. One Bitcoin equals 100,000,000 satoshis. Often used for micropayments, pricing, and stacking strategies, satoshis make it possible to transact in fractions of a Bitcoin bringing accessibility to everyday users in the decentralized economy.

Slippage - Medium Risk

The difference between expected and actual trade prices, especially during volatile market conditions or large transactions. Can be minimized on high-liquidity pools.

Smart Contract - Low Risk | Critical for 2028

Self-executing contracts with terms directly written into code. The foundation of all DeFi protocols, enabling trustless financial interactions.

Stablecoin - Low Risk | Critical for 2028

Cryptocurrencies designed to maintain stable value relative to a reference asset, usually the US Dollar. Examples: USDC, DAI, USDT. Essential for DeFi trading and lending.

Staking - Low Risk | Critical for 2028

Locking up tokens to support network security and earn rewards. Can be done natively on PoS blockchains or through liquid staking protocols like Lido.

Start9 - Low Risk | Critical for 2028

A sovereign computing platform that allows individuals to self-host essential internet services like websites, messaging, file storage, and Bitcoin nodes without relying on third parties. Start9's Embassy OS runs on devices like *Raspberry Pi* and supports decentralized protocols, empowering users with privacy, control, and full-stack ownership of their digital lives.

SushiSwap (SUSHI) - Low Risk

A community-owned *DEX* that forked from Uniswap, offering additional features like yield farming and governance token rewards.

T

Token - Low Risk | Critical for 2028

Digital assets built on existing blockchains. Can represent various things: currencies, governance rights, utility access, or ownership stakes.

Tokenomics - Low Risk | Critical for 2028

The economic model of a token, including supply, distribution, inflation rate, and utility. Critical for evaluating long-term investment potential.

TVL (Total Value Locked) - Low Risk | Critical for 2028

The total amount of assets locked in a DeFi protocol, indicating its popularity and liquidity. Higher TVL generally suggests greater trust and stability.

U

Uniswap (UNI) - Low Risk | Critical for 2028

The leading *decentralized exchange* that pioneered the *AMM* model. Features include concentrated liquidity and multi-chain deployment.

Un-staking - Low Risk

The process of withdrawing staked tokens, often subject to unbonding periods during which tokens cannot be accessed or transferred.

V

Vault - Low Risk | Critical

Smart contracts that automatically implement yield farming strategies. *Yearn Finance* vaults are popular for optimized, hands-off yield generation.

Volatility - Medium Risk

The degree of price variation in cryptocurrency markets. High volatility creates opportunities for traders but requires careful risk management.

W

Wallet - Low Risk | Critical for 2028

Software or hardware that stores private keys and enables cryptocurrency transactions. Essential for DeFi participation. See Chapter 10 for setup guide.

Web3 - Low Risk | Critical for 2028

The decentralized internet built on blockchain technology, enabling user ownership of data and assets. The foundation for the 2028 digital economy.

WBTC (Wrapped Bitcoin) - Low Risk | Critical for 2028

Bitcoin represented as an ERC-20 token on Ethereum, enabling Bitcoin holders to participate in DeFi protocols while maintaining Bitcoin exposure.

Whale - Medium Risk

Individuals or entities holding large amounts of cryptocurrency, capable of influencing market prices through their trading activities.

Whitepaper - Low Risk

Technical documents explaining a cryptocurrency project's technology, economics, and roadmap. Always read whitepapers before investing in new protocols.

X

X-Chain - Low Risk | Critical for 2028

Referring to cross-chain operations that span multiple blockchains. Essential for 2028 DeFi strategies that leverage multiple networks for optimization.

Y

Yearn Finance (YFI) - Low Risk | Critical for 2028

A yield optimization protocol that automatically moves funds between different DeFi protocols to maximize returns. Popular for passive yield generation.

Yggdrasil Encryption - Low Risk | Critical for 2028

A type of end-to-end encrypted communication used in the Yggdrasil Network, a decentralized mesh protocol built on IPv6. It allows devices to form secure, peer-to-peer connections without centralized servers, ensuring privacy and resilience across distributed systems.

Yggdrasil Protocol (Chain Abstraction Layer) - Low Risk | Critical for 2028

A modular infrastructure layer designed to unify settlement, execution, and permissioning across multiple blockchain ecosystems including Bitcoin, Ethereum, Solana, Cosmos, Move, and TON. Yggdrasil Protocol integrates data oracles, liquidity routing, cross-chain intents, and account abstraction into a single, streamlined stack. With built-in engines for data, aggregation, and abstraction, it eliminates fragmented infrastructure and improves cross-chain performance, composability, and simplicity across Web 3.0 networks.

Yield - Low Risk | Critical for 2028

The return earned on DeFi investments, typically expressed as Annual Percentage Yield (APY). Can come from lending, liquidity provision, or staking.

Yield Farming - Low Risk | Critical for 2028

The practice of moving funds between different DeFi protocols to maximize yield. Requires active management and understanding of protocol risks.

Example: Supplying USDC to Aave, borrowing against it, and farming rewards on multiple protocols simultaneously.

Yield Curve - Low Risk

A graph showing the relationship between interest rates and time to maturity. In DeFi, different protocols offer varying yields for different time commitments.

Z

Zero-Knowledge Proof - Medium Risk | Critical for 2028

Cryptographic methods that prove knowledge of information without revealing the information itself. Critical for privacy-preserving DeFi applications.

zk-SNARK - Medium Risk

A specific type of zero-knowledge proof that enables private transactions and computations. Used in privacy coins and scaling solutions.

zk-Rollup - Low Risk | Critical for 2028

Layer 2 scaling solution that bundles multiple transactions into a single proof, reducing costs while maintaining security. Expected to dominate by 2028.

Crypto Slang Terms: A Guide for the Curious

Ape In - Medium Risk

To invest quickly into a project (often without doing full research) based on hype or instinct.

Bag-holder - High Risk

Someone holding a cryptocurrency that's significantly dropped in value, hoping it will recover.

DAO - Low Risk

Decentralized Autonomous Organization; a community-led entity with no central leadership, governed by smart contracts.

Degen - High Risk

A bold, often experienced trader who dives into high-risk plays, yield farms, and meme tokens.

Diamond Hands - Medium Risk

A person who refuses to sell despite volatility, believing strongly in the asset.

Dust - Low Risk

Tiny leftover balances of cryptocurrency too small to trade or withdraw.

Exit Liquidity - High Risk

The latecomers who unknowingly buy a token at its peak, allowing early investors to cash out.

FOMO - High Risk

Fear Of Missing Out; an emotional reaction causing rushed buying during price surges.

FUD - High Risk

Fear, Uncertainty, and Doubt; often used to describe negative news or misinformation that causes panic.

Flippening - Medium Risk

The hypothetical event where another crypto (usually ETH) surpasses Bitcoin in market cap.

HODL - Low Risk

A misspelling of 'hold,' now a mantra for holding crypto long-term regardless of volatility.

NGMI - High Risk

Not Gonna Make It; used to describe bad decisions or lack of vision in crypto.

Paper Hands - High Risk

A trader who sells quickly during dips, unable to handle volatility.

Pump and Dump - Extreme Risk

A scheme where a coin is hyped to inflate price before insiders dump their holdings.

Rekt High - Risk

Slang for a heavy financial loss; often used humorously to describe liquidation.

Rug Pull - Extreme Risk

A scam where developers disappear with investors' funds, typically from a DeFi project.

Shill - Medium Risk

To promote a coin or project—sometimes dishonestly—for personal benefit.

To the Moon Speculative

A phrase expressing belief that an asset's price will skyrocket.

WAGMI - Low Risk

We're All Gonna Make It; a positive affirmation used in crypto communities.

Whale - Low Risk

An individual or entity holding a large amount of cryptocurrency, capable of influencing markets.

Essential DeFi Acronyms and Abbreviations

Quick Reference Guide:

APY: Annual Percentage Yield

AMM: Automated Market Maker

CEX: Centralized Exchange

DAO: Decentralized Autonomous Organization

DEX: Decentralized Exchange

DeFi: Decentralized Finance

EVM: Ethereum Virtual Machine

FOMO: Fear of Missing Out

FUD: Fear, Uncertainty, Doubt

HODL: Hold On for Dear Life

KYC: Know Your Customer

LP: Liquidity Provider

MEV: Maximal Extractable Value

NFT: Non-Fungible Token

OTC: Over-the-Counter

PoS: Proof of Stake

PoW: Proof of Work

TVL: Total Value Locked

WBTC: Wrapped Bitcoin

Common DeFi Protocol Names and Tickers

Major Protocols Reference:

AAVE: Aave lending protocol token

BAL: Balancer automated portfolio manager

COMP: Compound lending protocol token

CRV: Curve Finance stablecoin exchange

CVX: Convex Finance (Curve yield booster)

LINK: Chainlink oracle network token

MKR: MakerDAO governance token

SUSHI: SushiSwap decentralized exchange

UNI: Uniswap decentralized exchange

YFI: Yearn Finance yield optimizer

1INCH: 1inch DEX aggregator

Risk Assessment Terms

Understanding DeFi Risks:

Smart Contract Risk - High Risk: Bugs or exploits in protocol code

Liquidation Risk - High Risk: Automatic sale of collateral during price drops

Impermanent Loss - Medium Risk: Value loss from providing liquidity during price changes

Rug Pull Risk - High Risk: Developer abandonment and fund theft

Oracle Risk - Medium Risk: Manipulation or failure of price feeds

Regulatory Risk - Medium Risk: Government restrictions on protocols

Bridge Risk - Medium Risk: Cross-chain transfer vulnerabilities

Gas Risk - Medium Risk: High transaction fees during network congestion

2028 Strategic Terms

Essential for Future Positioning:

Bitcoin Halving - Critical for 2028: 2028 event reducing new Bitcoin supply

Institutional Adoption - Critical for 2028: Traditional finance entering DeFi

Regulatory Clarity - Critical for 2028: Clear legal frameworks for DeFi

Layer 2 Dominance - Critical for 2028: Scaling solutions becoming mainstream

Cross-Chain Interoperability - Critical for 2028: Seamless multi-blockchain operations

AI-DeFi Integration - Critical for 2028: Artificial intelligence optimizing DeFi strategies

Central Bank Digital Currencies: Government digital currencies potentially competing with DeFi

Quantum Resistance: Cryptographic protection against quantum computing threats

Mathematical and Technical Formulas

Key DeFi Calculations:

Constant Product Formula (Uniswap): $x \times y = k$

Compound Interest: $A = P(1 + r/n)^{(nt)}$

Impermanent Loss: $IL = 2\sqrt{(price\_ratio)} / (1 + price\_ratio) - 1$

Collateralization Ratio: $CR = Collateral\_Value / Loan\_Value$

Liquidation Price: $LP = Loan\_Amount \times Liquidation\_Ratio / Collateral\_Amount$

Annual Percentage Yield: APY = $(1 + r/n)^n - 1$

Price Impact: $PI = (Token\_Amount / Liquidity\_Pool) \times 100$

Understanding DeFi Math: Key Formulas Explained

For Readers Ready to Level Up

If you're serious about navigating the DeFi space like a true Jedi, understanding the math behind the systems is essential. Below are some of the most powerful formulas you'll encounter on your journey. Don't worry if they look intimidating at first mastery comes with practice, and we're here to break it all down.

Constant Product Formula (Uniswap): $x \times y = k$

Used to calculate how prices adjust in liquidity pools.

Compound Interest: $A = P(1 + r/n)^{(nt)}$

Understand how your crypto grows over time with compounding yield.

Impermanent Loss: $IL = 2\sqrt{(\text{price\_ratio})} / (1 + \text{price\_ratio}) - 1$

Shows the loss you may incur when providing liquidity instead of holding your assets.

Collateralization Ratio (CR): $CR = \text{Collateral\_Value} / \text{Loan\_Value}$

Measures how secure your position is in a DeFi loan.

Liquidation Price: $LP = \text{Loan\_Amount} \times \text{Liquidation\_Ratio} / \text{Collateral\_Amount}$

At this price, your collateral will be liquidated.

Annual Percentage Yield (APY): $APY = (1 + r/n)^n - 1$

Gives the actual yield after accounting for compounding interest.

Price Impact: $PI = (\text{Token\_Amount} / \text{Liquidity\_Pool}) \times 100$

Helps you avoid slippage when trading in small pools.

DeFi Jedi Tip: These formulas aren't just for traders or coders they're for freedom-minded individuals who want to see the game from the inside. Don't memorize them. Understand them.

In future editions, we'll break each one down visually with real-world examples and calculators to make it second nature.

Security and Best Practices Terms

Essential Security Concepts:

Multi-Signature Wallet: Requires multiple private keys to authorize transactions

Hardware Wallet: Physical devices storing private keys offline

Seed Phrase: 12-24 words that can recover your entire wallet

Private Key: Secret code proving ownership of cryptocurrency

Public Key: Address others can use to send you cryptocurrency

Cold Storage: Offline storage of cryptocurrency for maximum security

Hot Wallet: Online wallet for frequent transactions

Two-Factor Authentication: Additional security layer for account access

Phishing: Fraudulent attempts to steal login credentials

Social Engineering: Psychological manipulation to reveal sensitive information

Trading and Investment Terms

Market and Trading Concepts:

Market Cap: Total value of all tokens in circulation

Circulating Supply: Number of tokens currently available for trading

Market Maker: Entity providing liquidity by placing buy and sell orders

Market Taker: Entity removing liquidity by accepting existing orders

Spread: Difference between highest bid and lowest ask prices

Volume: Total amount of cryptocurrency traded over a period

OHLC: Open, High, Low, Close prices for a time period

Support Level: Price level where buying interest typically emerges

Resistance Level: Price level where selling pressure typically increases

Bull Trap: False signal suggesting price will continue rising

Bear Trap: False signal suggesting price will continue falling

Governance and DAO Terms

Decentralized Governance Concepts:

Proposal: Suggested changes to protocol parameters or features

Voting Power: Influence in governance decisions, typically based on token holdings

Quorum: Minimum participation required for valid governance decisions

Timelock: Delay between proposal approval and implementation

Veto Power: Ability to block proposals, often held by core teams

Delegate: Representative who votes on behalf of token holders

Snapshot: Platform for off-chain governance voting

Treasury: Protocol-controlled funds for development and operations

Working Group: Specialized teams focused on specific protocol aspects

How to Use This Glossary Effectively:

1. **Bookmark Key Terms:** Mark definitions you reference frequently
2. **Cross-Reference:** Follow italicized terms to build comprehensive understanding
3. **Risk Assessment:** Pay special attention to risk indicators (High Risk | Medium Risk | Low Risk)
4. **2028 Focus:** Prioritize terms marked with "Critical for 2028" for future positioning
5. **Regular Review:** Revisit definitions as you gain experience
6. **Practical Application:** Use terminology when researching new protocols

Remember: The DeFi landscape evolves rapidly. While these definitions provide a solid foundation, always verify current protocol mechanics and stay informed about new developments. This glossary serves as your reference point for understanding the complex but rewarding world of decentralized finance.

By mastering these terms and concepts, you'll be prepared to navigate the 2028 DeFi landscape with confidence and capitalize on the opportunities that await informed participants.

References and Resources

Official Government Sources

Congressional Bills and Legislation

GENIUS Act (S. 1582): "Guiding and Establishing National Innovation for U.S. Stablecoins Act" – Congress.gov

CLARITY Act (H.R. 3633): "Digital Asset Market Clarity Act of 2025" - Congress.gov

Anti-CBDC Surveillance State Act: Senate (S. 1124) / House (H.R. 1919) - Congress.gov

Infrastructure Investment and Jobs Act: Section 80603 Digital Asset Reporting - Congress.gov

Regulatory Bodies

Securities and Exchange Commission (SEC): www.sec.gov

Commodity Futures Trading Commission (CFTC): www.cftc.gov

Treasury Department: home.treasury.gov

Federal Reserve: www.federalreserve.gov

Academic and Research Sources

Web 3.0 and Blockchain Research

Ethereum Foundation: ethereum.org

MIT OpenCourseWare - Blockchain Technologies: ocw.mit.edu

Stanford Blockchain Research: cbr.stanford.edu

University of California Berkeley - Blockchain at Berkeley: blockchain.berkeley.edu

ConsenSys Academy: consensys.net/academy

Market Research and Analysis

Web 3.0 Market Analysis: Fortune Business Insights, Research and Markets, Grand View Research

DeFi Pulse: defipulse.com - DeFi protocol analytics

DeBank: debank.com - DeFi portfolio tracking

CoinMarketCap: coinmarketcap.com - Cryptocurrency data

CoinGecko: coingecko.com - Market analysis

Key DeFi Protocols and Platforms

Lending and Borrowing

Aave: aave.com - Decentralized lending protocol

Compound: compound.finance - Algorithmic money markets

MakerDAO: makerdao.com - DAI stablecoin protocol

Decentralized Exchanges (DEXs)

Uniswap: uniswap.org - Leading AMM protocol

PancakeSwap: pancakeswap.finance - BNB Chain DEX

1inch: 1inch.io - DEX aggregator

Yield Farming and Asset Management

Yearn Finance: yearn.fi - Yield optimization

Convex Finance: convexfinance.com - Curve yield booster

Enzyme Finance: enzyme.finance - Asset management

Technical Resources and Documentation

Blockchain Development

Ethereum Developer Resources: ethereum.org/developers

Solidity Documentation: docs.soliditylang.org

OpenZeppelin: openzeppelin.com - Smart contract security

Chainlink: chain.link - Oracle network documentation

Web 3.0 Infrastructure

IPFS (InterPlanetary File System): ipfs.io

Filecoin: filecoin.io - Decentralized storage

The Graph: thegraph.com - Indexing protocol

Polkadot: polkadot.network - Multi-chain protocol

Security and Risk Management

Smart Contract Auditing

ConsenSys Diligence: consensys.net/diligence

Trail of Bits: trailofbits.com

OpenZeppelin Security: openzeppelin.com/security-audits

Hardware Wallets and Security

Ledger: ledger.com - Hardware wallet solutions

Trezor: trezor.io - Hardware wallet security

MetaMask: metamask.io - Browser wallet

News and Industry Analysis

Cryptocurrency News

CoinDesk: coindesk.com

The Block: theblock.co

Decrypt: decrypt.co

Cointelegraph: cointelegraph.com

DeFi and Web 3.0 Analysis

DeFi Llama: defillama.com - TVL and protocol analytics

Dune Analytics: dune.com - Blockchain data analysis

Messari: messari.io - Crypto research

Legal and Compliance Resources

Legal Analysis

Cooper & Kirk: Legal analysis of Operation Choke Point 2.0

Coin Center: coincenter.org - Cryptocurrency policy research

Blockchain Association: theblockchainassociation.org

Tax and Compliance

IRS Virtual Currency Guidance: irs.gov

CoinTracker: cointracker.io - Tax compliance tools

TaxBit: taxbit.com - Enterprise crypto tax

Educational Resources for Further Study

Online Courses and Certifications

Coursera - Blockchain Specialization: University of Buffalo

edX - Introduction to Blockchain: UC Berkeley

Udemy - Ethereum and Solidity: Various instructors

ConsenSys Academy: Professional blockchain certification

Books and Publications

"Mastering Bitcoin" by Andreas M. Antonopoulos

"Mastering Ethereum" by Andreas M. Antonopoulos and Gavin Wood

"The Infinite Machine" by Camila Russo

"DeFi and the Future of Finance" by Campbell Harvey, Ashwin Ramachandran, and Joey Santoro

Key Figures and Thought Leaders

Vitalik Buterin: Ethereum co-founder - @VitalikButerin

Gavin Wood: Polkadot founder, Web3 Foundation

Hayden Adams: Uniswap founder

Stani Kulechov: Aave founder

Andre Cronje: Yearn Finance architect

Tools and Analytics Platforms

Etherscan: etherscan.io - Ethereum blockchain explorer

Tenderly: tenderly.co - Smart contract monitoring

Zapper: zapper.fi - DeFi portfolio management

Zerion: zerion.io - DeFi wallet and analytics

Disclaimer

The information provided in this book and the resources listed are for educational purposes only. Cryptocurrency investments carry significant risks, including the potential loss of principal. Always conduct your own research and consult with qualified financial and legal professionals before making investment decisions. The regulatory landscape continues to evolve rapidly, and readers should verify current laws and regulations in their jurisdiction.

The author and publisher are not responsible for any losses or damage resulting from the use of information contained in this book or from accessing the resources listed. All URLs and references were accurate at the time of publication but may change over time.

Conclusion

The DeFi landscape in 2025 presents unprecedented opportunities for informed participants. With improving regulatory clarity, enhanced security practices, and maturing protocols, intermediate users can navigate this space with greater confidence.

Success in DeFi requires:

- Continuous learning and adaptation
- Rigorous risk management
- Regulatory compliance awareness
- Community engagement
- Technical competence

The Decentralized Sovereign Network represents a vision of financial freedom through technological empowerment. By combining education, community, and practical applications, participants can build wealth while contributing to a more decentralized future.

Disclaimer

This material is for educational purposes only and should not be construed as financial advice. Cryptocurrency investments carry significant risks, including the potential loss of principal. Always conduct your own research and consult with qualified financial professionals before making investment decisions.

The regulatory landscape for DeFi continues to evolve rapidly. Users should stay informed about current regulations in their jurisdiction to ensure compliance with all applicable laws.

Smart contract risks, including bugs, exploits, and governance failures, remain significant concerns in the DeFi space. Never invest more than you can afford to lose, and always prioritize security over potential returns.

About the Author

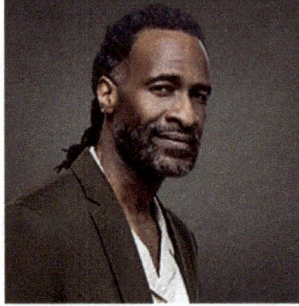

Founder of Bit Main Street, creator of Satoshi For Storage, and a man on a mission to help everyday people become extraordinary through the power of decentralized technology.

With over 25 years of experience as a full-stack .NET developer, I've spent my life building digital systems that break boundaries not reinforce them.

My journey began in the Bay Area, where I sharpened my technical craft in Silicon Valley during the early web revolution. That journey took me across the world, where I worked with global financial institutions like Saxo Bank and Citigroup in Copenhagen, Denmark, helping to develop high-performance digital platforms that powered international banking operations.

I'm also a certified martial artist trained in Peace Power Qigong under Master Fan Xiulan, a practice rooted in discipline, energy, and focus. The same principles that guide my physical training fuel my approach to technology: precision, balance, and respect for the unseen forces at play. Whether in the dojo or the digital world, my aim has always been the same: liberation through mastery.

Over the years, I've grown from full stack developer to crypto educator, entrepreneur, and community builder. I founded the Crypto Academy and launched the Bit Main Street Network to empower entrepreneurs with tools, training, and decentralized solutions that actually work. My clients aren't just learning; they're transforming their businesses into sovereign ecosystems.

One of my proudest innovations is Satoshi For Storage, a privacy-first, Bitcoin-powered file hosting system that combines IPFS security with Lightning payments. No surveillance. No middlemen. Just speed, freedom, and control: the way the internet was always meant to be.

If you're ready to be transformed, then your teacher has arrived, and I've never backed down from the truth.

Read more at David James Green's site.

www.ingramcontent.com/pod-product-compliance
Lightning Source LLC
Chambersburg PA
CBHW071332210326
41597CB00015B/1429